Pewter Jewellery

Pewter Jewellery

Miriam Browne

B T Batsford Limited
Van Nostrand Reinhold   Australia   Melbourne

To Peter, Rowena, Chris and Mick, with love

ISBN 0 7134 1608 4 (U.K.)

ISBN 0-442-25011-8 (Australia)

Filmset in 'Monophoto' Plantin by
Servis Filmsetting Ltd, Manchester
Printed by The Anchor Press Ltd
of Tiptree, Essex
for the publishers B T Batsford Ltd
4 Fitzhardinge Street, London W1H 0AH
and Van Nostrand Reinhold
17 Queen Street, Mitcham
Victoria 3132

Contents

Acknowledgment

I would like to thank the following people and organizations for their help in supplying illustrations and information:

Ian Anderson, Director of The College of Craft Education Summer School at West Dean; Sue Blackman, engraver; British Museum; Cowes Library; Diane Doubtfire, author; Dr Dean of the Tin Research Institute; Mike Edwards, photographer; Nigel Edmondson, artist, lecturer and artistic adviser; Fareham Library; David Harkison, pewtersmith, Harkison Jewellery, Glasgow; Jean Pierre Massart, pewtersmith; Nottingham Castle Museum; Students at West Dean: Susan O Coelho, Ron Cooper, Mike Hylton, Ray Jones, Donald Matheson, Stan Morgan, June Pettersson, Rosemary Rey, Elizabeth Tindall; The Guildhall Library, London; The Museum of London; The Worshipful Company of Pewterers.

The courtesy and help of the firms who supplied me with materials and information is greatly appreciated. I would like to express special gratitude to Nigel Edmondson, for his help, encouragement and for allowing me to use so much of his work. I am also indebted to my friend and photographer, Mike Edwards, for his patience and forbearance. My thanks also go to Pauline Stride of B T Batsford for her help and cooperation during the compiling of the manuscript.

Introduction

This book has been written to help to stimulate the renewed interest which is already being shown in pewter throughout the world. Hours of relaxation and satisfaction can be obtained by developing traditional or original ideas, and using pewter to produce individual pieces of jewellery for personal use or for profit.

All the methods discussed in this book have been thoroughly tested, and only those processes which can be worked in a comparatively small space and which require little capital outlay have been included in any detail. People who have a special room which they can devote to the craft are fortunate, but many talents would remain untapped if all art and craft work had to be carried out in a fully equipped studio.

Figure 1 : Pewter bracelets, pendants, brooches and cuff links modelled in relief.

The tools required for making pewter jewellery do not involve great expense, in fact, many of them can be found around the home, or can be produced by a handyman, or an enthusiast in a school workshop. As a metal, pewter is versatile and can be used in a number of different ways. It can be beaten and raised to form attractive designs. It also lends itself to casting, etching and, having such a low melting point, it is easy to solder.

For those people who are at first unable to design and produce individual ideas, this book contains projects to follow and designs to copy, but it is hoped that the contents of the book will develop an awareness of the variety of ideas which can be seen every day, and will open up new fields of interest which will stimulate the imagination of the would-be pewtersmith.

Pewter is a comfortable metal to work with and, even though it will never attain the durability and value of gold, silver and platinum, it will nevertheless command respect if it is worked properly and allowed to reveal the special charm embodied within it. The 'ethnic' quality of pewter imparts a certain strength of character to the work which goes deeper than the design itself, while the 'antique feel' of the metal lends itself to simple motifs taken from early or primitive cultures.

It is a superb metal for the jeweller to work with, in both the amateur and professional fields, and it is hoped that the ideas and illustrations in this book will provide a rich source of inspiration for the beginner and the experienced craftsman.

The Heritage of Pewter

The History of the Metal

The origins of the craft of the pewtersmith are lost in obscurity. It is a craft belonging to a romantic past, and its secrets were guarded and surrounded by an aura of mystique.

The composition of the metal has varied considerably throughout the ages. The Romans were known to have used as much as thirty per cent of lead in their pewter. They were obviously unaware of the high toxicity produced in such an alloy and totally unconcerned with health and safety!

During and after the Roman occupation, the craft spread to the Netherlands, Germany, Spain, Scandinavia and France. It is recorded that a craft guild of pewterers existed in France, near the Bordeaux region, as early as the eleventh century, but by the early Middle Ages England had undoubtedly become the pewter centre of the medieval world, and it was at this time that reputable craftsmen banded together in groups, to protect their craft, to insist upon certain standards of workmanship and to maintain the quality of the pewter being sold.

Three categories of pewter were being marketed, a pure metal, known as 'English Pewter', a test pewter and a low-grade pewter. English pewter was made of tin and copper, or tin and antimony with sometimes a little bismuth added. This was the best quality, and since it contained no lead, it was by far the most expensive. Test pewter contained lead, which made it more malleable and pliable, and it was widely used despite its lower-grade quality.

The unscrupulous and dishonest craftsman would add more and more lead, thus producing a metal which was cheap to manufacture but which might be sold at prices which would give profits. It was a heavy metal, and quickly turned an unattractive blackish grey colour.

9

In 1348 a group of pewter craftsmen in London banded together to form The Worshipful Company of Pewterers of London. A charter was granted to them in 1473 by Edward IV, which hangs to this day in the hall of the present Company in Oat Lane. The charter gave the right of search and inspection. It enabled the quality of the metal to be controlled, and any craftsmen discovered using inferior pewter was in danger of having his work seized and his reputation destroyed. So thorough were the controls exercised that until 1673 English pewter enjoyed an unrivalled reputation.

By 1650, the craft of pewtersmithing had spread to America, although Britain was still relied upon to supply the industry with tin. The demand for pewter increased and the craft enjoyed great prosperity and popularity from 1750 to 1850.

It was about 1750 that a pewter known as Britannia Metal was introduced. This was an alloy of tin, which contained a small amount of antimony, but no lead; it became highly desirable because of its more durable qualities and its brighter appearance.

After 1850, the availability of cheaper utensils and tableware, in the form of china, lead to a rapid decline in the popularity of pewter for everyday use. Yet today the pewter industry is once again enjoying renewed worldwide interest. Modern pewter is essentially a twentieth-century material, and the standard of its manufacture can be guaranteed. It is available in sheet and ingot form, and is becoming an increasingly popular material for the amateur and professional craftsman to work into jewellery and other decorative pieces as well as tableware.

Pewter Jewellery through the Ages

A pewter 'pilgrim's bottle' found at Abydos in Egypt, dated approximately 1500BC – probably the oldest piece of pewter known to archaeologists – is proof that the metal was known to the Pharaohs. Yet, knowing their love of gold and precious stones, it is not surprising that further research has revealed little sign of pewter jewellery connected with that period of history. The poorer people might have used the metal for their own body ornaments, but this is only conjecture.

During the Roman occupation of Europe, it is known that the peoples of the Empire were familiar with a type of pewter which contained a very high percentage of lead. The only pieces to have survived are utensils and bowls. No pewter jewellery which could be attributed to the Romans has been found, so once again it is probable that they considered the metal to be for utilitarian needs only and not suitable for ornamental use.

The Anglo Saxons, despite favouring gold, silver and bronze for jewellery making, were known to have cast brooches in pewter. However, records state that these were poorly designed and not particularly well made. A single Saxon cruciform brooch, made of pewter, discovered in Reading, was probably a piece of experimental casting, produced from metal obtained from a local source.

The most comprehensive and by far the most interesting find of early

pewter jewellery to be discovered is the collection now known as the
Cheapside Hoard (figure 2), which is now kept in The Museum of
London. This is a hoard of eleventh-century cheap pewter and silver
jewellery found in Cheapside, which was at that time the site of West
Cheap, one of the two main trading areas in the City of London – the
other one being East Cheap, where Cannon Street is today. The hoard
was probably the stock of a jeweller. Some of the pieces remain un-
finished, whilst others are freshly cast and awaiting final cleaning and
polishing.

It is interesting to note that an exact replica of the largest brooch
discovered in Cheapside was found in Dublin (figure 3). This shows
that there was an obvious trading link and that pewter jewellery was not
unknown in Ireland.

During the thirteenth, fourteenth and fifteenth centuries the pilgrimage enjoyed enormous popularity. These medieval expeditions allowed people from all walks of life to visit holy shrines in cheerful company, protected from the perils which frequently beset the lone traveller. The pilgrims visited shrines throughout Britain, Europe, and the Holy Land. Signs or badges made of pewter, cast in stone or iron moulds, were sold at the shrines and worn by the pilgrims as proof of their visits.

> *Then, as manere and custom is, signes there they bought,*
> *For men of contré should know whom they had sought.*
> (From the Supplement to *The Canterbury Tales*, Chaucer)

Sometimes they wore their talismen round their necks, but more often they were pinned onto a hat.

> *Ye may se by my signes*
> *That sitten on myn hatte.*
> (From Langland's *Vision of Piers Plowman*, c.1360–1400)

Figure 4: A selection of pilgrim's badges found in the River Thames
(a) The head of a horse
(b) A chained swan found at Swan Pier
(c) A badge in the shape of a scallop shell depicting a pilgrim wearing a wide brimmed hat (found at London Bridge)
(d) A small badge with a pin still in tact on the reverse side, found at Swan Pier
(e) An incomplete cast mitred head, within a circular frame, set with circles and diamonds, found in the Thames at Dowgate

A great number of these pewter badges have survived and have been found in the River Thames (figure 4a, b, c, d, e). Not all of them are complete, but those which have survived portray a variety of subjects. Some show the Virgin and Child, whilst others show subjects as varied as a mitred head, a shell, a chained swan, the head of a horse or just a simple, raised scrolled design.

a

b

c

d
e

The badges of St Thomas of Canterbury deserve a special mention. Many examples are to be found in the British Museum, the Museum of London, and the Musée de Cluny in Paris. Many of these show a mitred head, or a mitred figure on horseback. Perhaps the most unusual badge is that which is known as a pewter Canterbury Bell (figure 5), which was sold as a curio at the shrine of the abbey bearing its name.

It is interesting to note that in France, clasps and brooches of pewter were worn by the less-wealthy to decorate their hats, shoes and clothes. Records show that these were often political badges worn during the uprisings in 1358 and 1411.

From the Middle Ages to the seventeenth century very little pewter jewellery is recorded, but it is known that during the 1600s the Norwegians favoured eyelets cast from pewter to decorate the edges of their bodices. This trend continued into the following century, when cast-pewter buttons became fashionable. Pewter fastenings and decorations on thick knit garments are still used today (figure 8).

Figure 5 : A pewter 'Canterbury Bell', sold as a curio

Figure 6 : A shoe buckle, probably fifteenth-century

Figure 8 : Pewter eyelet on a felt and wool jacket, lavishly embroidered with brightly coloured yarns of turquoise, red, yellow and royal blue (courtesy June Pettersson)

Figure 7 : Toy pewter watch, c.1700 (courtesy The Museum of London

*Figure 9 : Close up of cast
pewter eyelet illustrated in
figure 8 (courtesy June
Pettersson)*

*Figure 10 : A hat pin and hair
comb of tortoiseshell which are
both decorated with 'stones'
which appear to be made of
glass (courtesy Nottingham
Castle Museum)*

A considerable amount of pewter, mainly hammered and worked in relief, belonging to the early twentieth century, is to be found in museums and second-hand shops. A particularly interesting collection of pewter jewellery probably dating around 1910 is shown in figures 10, 11, 12 and 13. These are all part of a collection which used to belong to Mr Edgar Hutchinson, who had a pewter workshop in Dryden Street, Nottingham, pre-1914. The stones he used were doubtless locally produced by the Ruskin Pottery (W Howson Taylor, Smethwick, near Birmingham, 1898 to 1935). Besides jewellery, Mr Hutchinson made a number of pewter goods for sale both locally and for outlets in London.

With the resurgence of worldwide interest in pewter and the technological advances which have taken place in the production of a more durable metal, perhaps much of what the small craftsman creates today will one day be 'discovered' and considered to be of historical value!

Figure 11 : A single brooch, 80 mm (3⅛ in) long, showing a fine ceramic stone of mottled green, blue and yellow, probably made by the Ruskin Pottery (courtesy Nottingham Castle Museum)

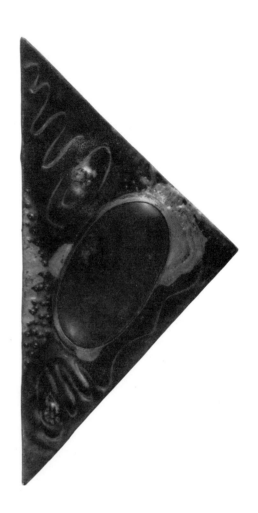

Figure 12 : The triangular brooch has a mottled deep, pink stone, probably Ruskin, whilst the circular brooch has a mottled blue stone. What appears to be the original sale tag is attached to the back of the circular brooch : 15/6d (courtesy Nottingham Castle Museum)

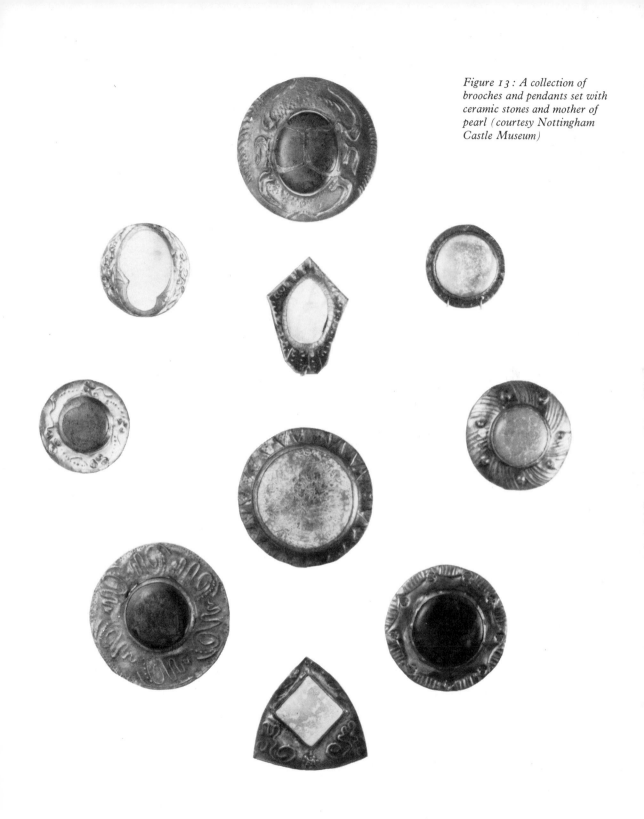

Figure 13 : A collection of brooches and pendants set with ceramic stones and mother of pearl (courtesy Nottingham Castle Museum)

Modern Pewter

Composition of the Metal

What is pewter? What is it made of? These are questions which are frequently asked. A great deal of curiosity still surrounds its composition and many people find it difficult to accept the absence of quantities of lead in most alloys. If lead is used at all, it is limited to .05% of its total composition.

Pewter is a timeless metal. Technologists are constantly researching to produce more perfect alloys in order to fulfil present-day requirements. Manufacturers and individual craftsmen alike demand not only pewter for casting but also sheet pewter of varying thicknesses. It must be suitable for relief work, for hammering, soldering and etching. The correct physical and mechanical properties of the resulting alloy make all these techniques possible.

An alloy is produced by melting and fusing together a number of metals, which, when allowed to solidify, form one metal. In the case of modern pewter, the proportions of the metals which form the alloy are approximately 92% tin, 6% antimony and 2% copper. If a slightly harder pewter is required, a small percentage of bismuth or cadmium is

Figure 14: A micro-photograph taken at the Tin Research Institute, showing at high magnification the structure of a modern pewter alloy (courtesy Tin Research Institute)

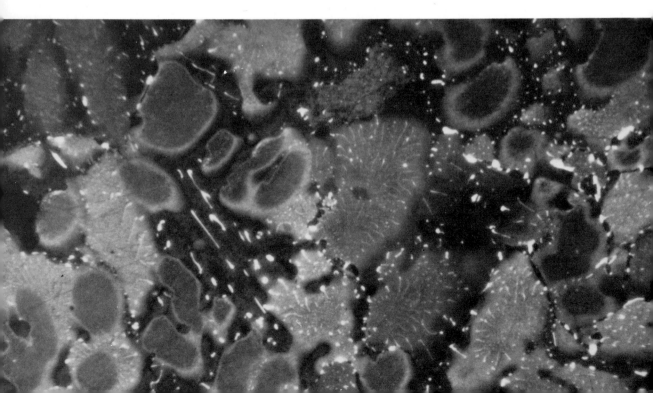

added. With or without the bismuth, the metal is eminently suitable for the making of jewellery.

The alloy produced is eutectic, that is, it melts at a lower temperature than any of its components. Tin melts at $231.89°C$ ($449.42°F$). Antimony melts at $630.5°C$ ($1,166.9°F$) and copper melts at $1,083°C$ ($1,981.4°F$). The melting point of pewter is between $218.3°C$ to $226.6°C$ ($425°F$ to $440°F$). The metals used in the above quantities produce an alloy more ductile and malleable than virtually any other metal. Its advantageous characteristics are numerous.

Tin, which forms by far the greater part of the alloy, is very brittle when used by itself, so to counteract this fault and to prevent it from cracking and splitting whilst it is being worked, antimony is added. The latter also contributes a degree of hardness to the pewter. The 2% of copper is used to give it the necessary ductility and malleability to ensure that the pewter is workable. Ductility enables the metal to be stretched and pulled in all directions without cracking. Malleability enables the pewter to be hammered, beaten, pressed and bent into practically any shape without damaging the appearance or the structure of the metal.

When being hammered or subjected to pressure, pewter does not 'work harden' and consequently, unlike gold, silver and copper, never requires annealing. If a metal does work harden it becomes brittle, and to prevent it from cracking it has to be annealed, that is, heated and cooled, in order to restore it to a malleable and ductile condition. The tenacity or tensile strength of pewter is such that it enables the stretching and pressing processes to take place without fracturing the composition of the metal.

Yet another great advantage which makes pewter a popular material for jewellery is the ease with which it can be cast. Its low melting point and its high fluidity when molten make it ideal for all methods of casting, using either simple inexpensive equipment or sophisticated modern machinery.

Pewter can be soldered, but because of its very low melting point, care must be taken not to overheat the metal, otherwise the result can be disastrous. Most metals produce oxides during the soldering process and as a result have to be chemically cleaned or pickled. This is not so, however, in the case of pewter. The only oxide-producing metal present in its composition is the small proportion of copper, which does not produce sufficient oxides to necessitate cleaning.

It must by now be apparent that the pewter produced by modern technology is a metal which richly deserves the interest it now commands. It no longer automatically turns a dull grey colour, but retains its silver sheen and high lustre, which looks good when used in conjunction with other materials, such as wood, leather, thread and semi-precious stones. It can, however, be artificially darkened to give it the appearance of antique pewter.

The Tin Research Institute is continually striving to ensure that, despite the growth in the pewter industry, and the development of mass

Figure 15 : Alloying, pewter
slabs of controlled quality are
the raw materials of the
pewterer (courtesy Tin
Research Institute)

production, the quality of the metal will not decline. For should supplies of tin become scarce throughout the world, the jewellery we make today might suddenly become valuable and a fashionable commodity to collect!

Quality marks (touchmarks)

Modern Pewter Associations and Pewter Guilds are anxious to ensure that manufacturers maintain high standards and only use pewter which meets the required specifications for metal content. For this purpose the touchmark of a craftsman can be regarded as the best guarantee of quality. Quality marks are stamped onto pewterware and sales tags throughout Britain, the United States of America and West Germany.

Many European manufacturers, especially those operating in Belgium, are being persuaded to join the associations which have been and are being formed in their respective countries. This should ensure that pewter bought throughout the world is of a universal quality.

Cleaning pewter jewellery

Modern pewter can be cleaned by washing it in warm, soapy water and rubbing it with a soft cloth. If a piece of jewellery has become extremely finger marked, grease remover or silver polish can be used sparingly before washing the article. Strong detergents and gritty polishing mediums should never be used.

Pewter Jewellery of Today

Pewter jewellery is usually classified as high-quality costume jewellery. Its value falls between silver and the trinket-type of mass-produced bauble seen in many gift shop windows. However, some of the better-designed pieces of work do command prices equal to those paid for silver.

Figure 16 : A pendant from the interesting 'Essence' jewellery from Sweden (courtesy Tin Research Institute)

*Figure 17 : Emblems of
Scotland are translated into
Design Council Award-
winning pendants by David
Harkison of Glasgow (courtesy
Tin Research Institute)*

Some manufacturers are mass producing ranges of popular designs, but the standard of workmanship is high and the content of the pewter used, in most cases, is checked at source, to ensure that the jewellery produced meets with the standards laid down by the Modern Pewter Associations.

Despite mass production, much of the jewellery available today still remains highly individual and exclusive, because each item is handmade. Even when using the same design idea, it is practically impossible to create two articles which are exactly alike in every detail.

Artists throughout the world, in Scandinavia, the United States of America, Europe and Australia, are today producing highly individual work. The jewellery ranges from delicate and intricate designs to pieces with bold and elegant lines. Without a doubt pewter has a worldwide appeal. The availability of magazines, trade journals, trade exhibitions and of the experimental work being done by the International Tin Research Councils – all these things are helping to promote a renewed interest in pewter as a material for jewellery.

Although some of the work for sale still echoes the designs of a richly romantic past, the field is wide open for experimentation. Contemporary designs and ideas are needed to complement the fashion trends of today. It is inevitable that more advanced methods of manufacture will be increasingly introduced to make pewter more easily available, but there is always a place for the craftsman to experiment, and to produce unique and individual works of art.

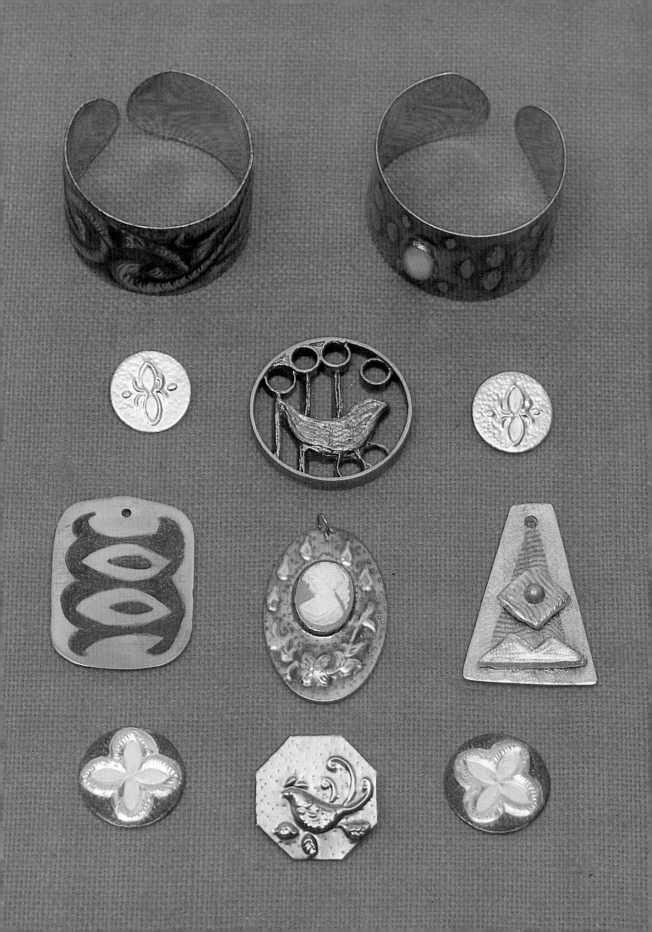

Design

A thing of beauty is a joy for ever. Keats

When confronted by a piece of raw pewter, whether it be in sheet, scrap or slab form, the craftsman must first work out the basic design before a piece of jewellery can be produced. There are numerous books devoted entirely to design, and many people reading this book will already have had a thorough training in the subject, but for the benefit of those readers who find it difficult to think of ideas quickly, this chapter will act as a stimulus, to encourage them to experiment, and help them be aware of ideas which can be seen every day.

Ideas abound in the home: ornaments, soft furnishings, fabrics, floor coverings, wallpaper and cushions are all potential sources for design ideas (figures 18 to 24).

Figure 18 : A small ornament such as this silver candlestick, can act as the starting point for a design.

Figure 19 : Drawing based on the candlestick.

Figure 20 : The fish, worked in relief

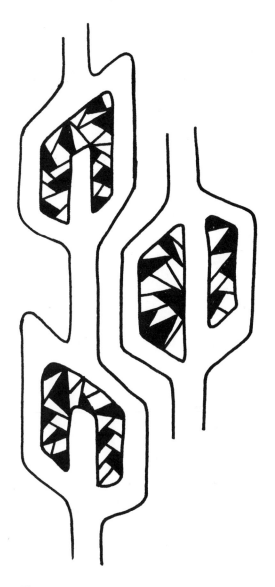

Figure 21 : This idea originated from a soft furnishing fabric

Figure 22 : (right) Three ideas inspired by the fabric

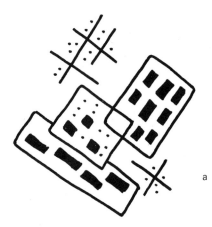

Figure 23 : Ideas obtained from
lino floor covering

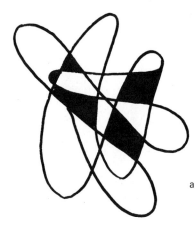

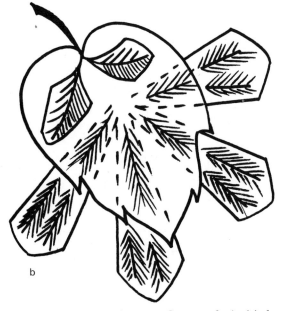

Figure 24 : Ideas inspired by
wall coverings

Figure 25 : Design for a bangle

The garden and countryside with its landscapes, flowers, fruit, birds and insects, also provide constantly changing ideas (figures 25 to 28).

A visit to the shore and a brief study of a rock pool will inspire many interesting design shapes and encourage the imagination to invent recognizable or abstract forms (figures 29 to 32).

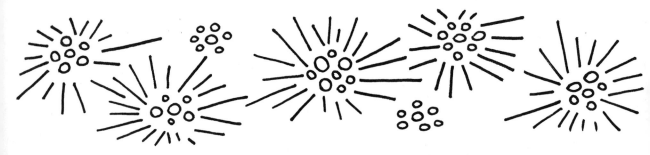

Figure 26 : Jewellery designs stolen from nature

Figure 27 : (left) Designs for pendants or brooches

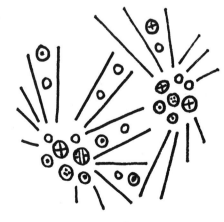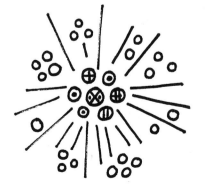

29

Figure 28 : The garden offers numerous ideas, many of which can be translated into pewter

Figure 29 A collection of shells providing curved, ridged and spiral forms

Figure 30 : Shell designs may be simple or complex

Figure 31 : Stylized designs can be taken from marine life forms

Figure 32 : Simplified boat shapes make a balanced composition

31

Books are a constant fount of inspiration, especially those dealing with primitive cultures, or the early civilizations in Egypt and Greece. If, on the other hand, one is searching for tangible evidence of the past, there is no better place than a museum. Many libraries will obtain catalogues on request, showing photographic records of famous art treasures, collections and exhibitions (figures 33 to 35).

Often, just putting pencil to paper and forming ovals, circles, curves or just a series of lines, can result in shapes which are pleasant to look at (figures 36 and 37).

Figure 33 : Drawing of a bangle which was made after browsing through a book on Greek mythology

Figure 34 : Drawings made after reading a book based on the Jivaro tribe of South America

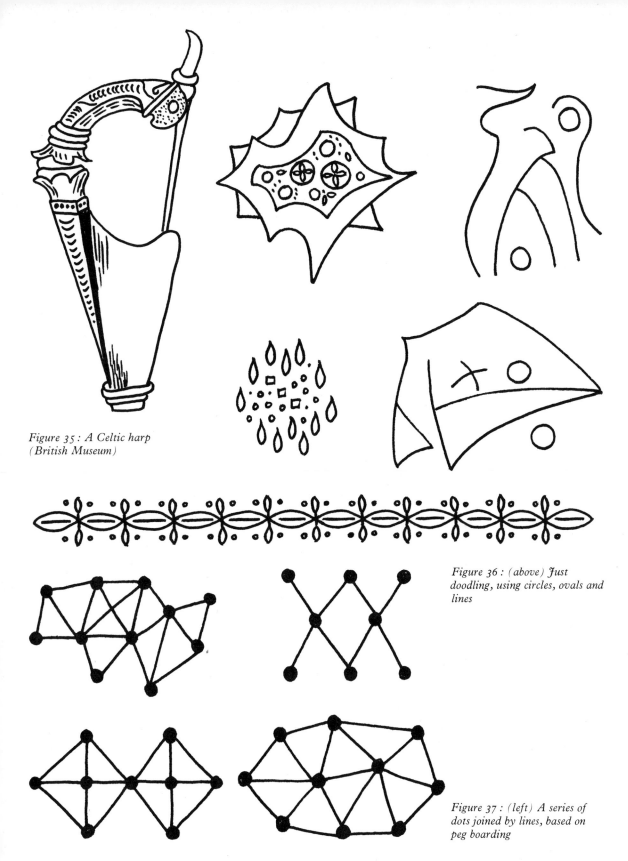

Figure 35 : A Celtic harp
(British Museum)

Figure 36 : (above) Just
doodling, using circles, ovals and
lines

Figure 37 : (left) A series of
dots joined by lines, based on
peg boarding

33

It must be remembered that when looking at drawings in books or patterns on fabrics, these are designs of a two-dimensional nature. When creating a piece of jewellery, this is essentially a three-dimensional object, because the length, breadth and thickness of the article must be considered. For the designer who finds it impossible to imagine a drawing as anything other than a flat thing, it is helpful to create a model in plasticine or wax. If this method fails to produce successful results, it is perhaps wiser to base one's ideas for designs upon articles which are themselves of a three-dimensional nature.

Having thought of an idea, it is important to remember that the design must have shape and form and be arranged in such a way that it is pleasing to the eye. Contrast, colour and texture must also be considered.

Because pewter is capable of undergoing a number of processes, and of being worked in completely different ways, many of the designs used for the varying techniques will alter considerably in the making. Some ideas can be adapted to suit more than one technique, for example, the fish, worked in relief and cut out ready for mounting, is equally successful when cast, using a random type dot and line design (figure 38).

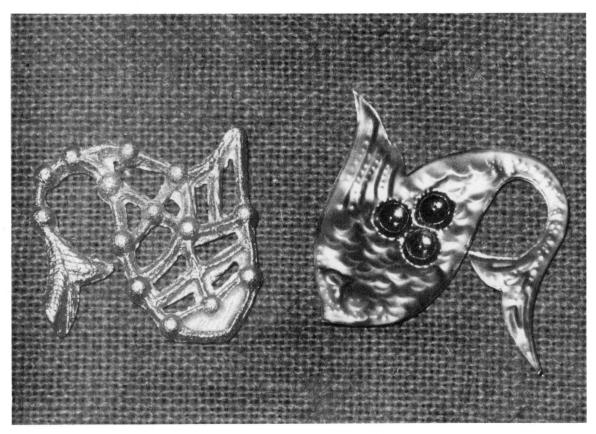

Figure 38 : The same drawing of a fish (see figure 31) has been used for relief work and for cuttlefish casting to produce different effects

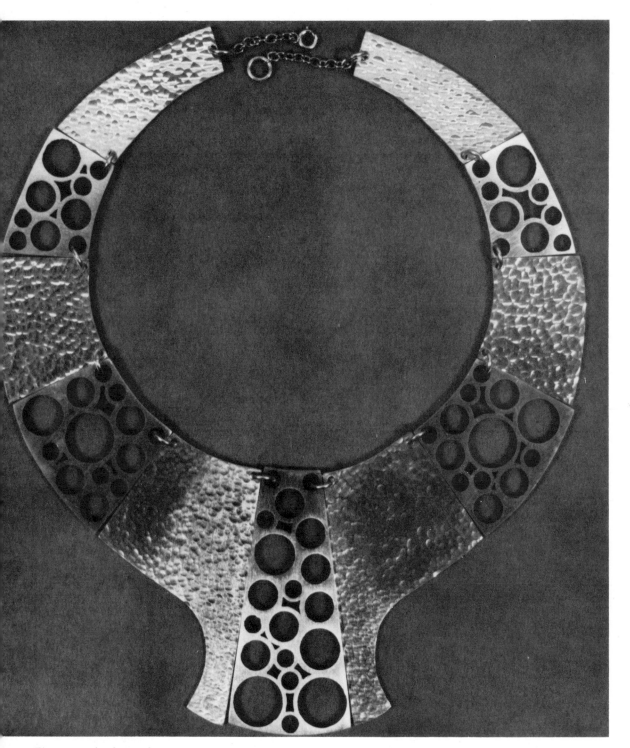

*Figure 39 : An eleven-piece
pewter necklace of perfect
symmetry showing a combination
of pierced elements, cast in
cuttlefish bone, and hammer-
textured sheet pewter (courtesy
Nigel Edmondson)*

35

Thought must be given to the type of jewellery being designed, and an important consideration is its weight. A chunky cast pendant, with bold, imaginative lines, slung on a chain would be fine, but the same idea used for earrings, if not modified, would result in oversize, unwieldy objects, which would weigh too heavily on the ear lobes! A brooch or tie pin must also be light enough and smooth enough not to drag, snag or stretch the garment upon which it is pinned.

When considering shape, one must decide whether the design is going to be unconventional and abstract in form, or regular and symmetrical. The necklace in figure 39 shows undisputed symmetry. If divided through the centre, the two halves show perfect balance and are alike in shape and size, producing an object of exact proportions and absolute harmony.

Silhouettes can be used to advantage when etching, where a lighter surround is left to complement the wholly blackened areas of the design.

They can also be used to advantage, where the silhouette forms the

Figure 40 : The silhouette of a tree used to great effect – the same idea has been exploited to create more than one pendant (courtesy Nigel Edmondson)

outline of the design, as in the case of the pendants (figure 40). Here one can also see a perfect example of one idea leading to another.

When working with pewter, visual contrast can readily be obtained. This is easily achieved when casting with cuttlefish bone. The bone itself produces superb curves which in turn, if left unpolished, give unrivalled textural effects (figure 41). Where parts of a design are subsequently polished, the difference between light and shade are increased, resulting in even greater interest (figure 40).

Colour can be introduced by using pewter patina, which also gives the illusion of depth, or by using gold leaf decoration. Stones, thread, wood and leather are other materials which can be incorporated to produce colour contrast.

Often the combination of two different techniques to produce composite jewellery can be used to great effect, for example, casting and soldering, or casting and hammering (figures 42, 43).

Vulgarity and over-ornamentation can destroy good design, whether

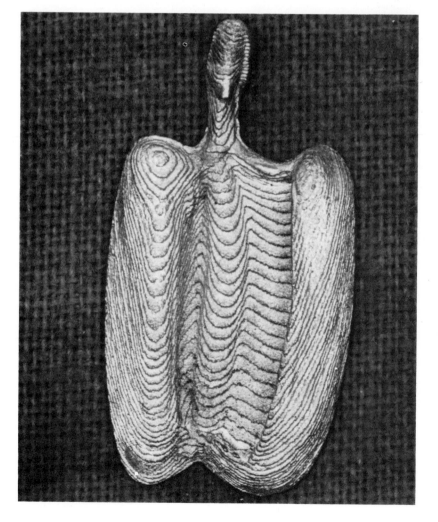

Figure 41 : The curves of the cuttlefish bone, showing perfect texture (courtesy Susan O. Coelho

37

it be abstract or representational. A certain degree of constraint must be observed and the desire to be outrageous, just to be different, controlled. Pewter is at its most attractive when fashioned into simple, classic shapes, with uncluttered lines. It lends itself to a variety of finishes, from a bright silver lustre to a dull velvety satin, and to a variety of textures, from a smooth, reflective, high polish to a beaten, bark-like finish hinting at creases and shadows.

The subdued effects which can be produced team well with the type of fashion colours in vogue today. Pewter never looks garish and cheap. It is a metal worthy of the finest design.

Figure 42: Combining techniques: an eleven-piece necklace, showing pierced elements cast in cuttlefish bone, and hammer-textured sheet pewter (courtesy Nigel Edmondson)

Figure 43 : A ring showing a combination of techniques, casting and soldering (courtesy Nigel Edmondson)

Modelling in Relief

The Basic Technique

Using the pewter and the tools which are available today for modelling in relief, this quite justifiably qualifies as a twentieth-century craft. During the past few years, it has become increasingly popular. Although tools can be bought specifically for this technique, there is tremendous scope for improvization with a whole range of implements. If a tool can impress the sheet pewter in a neat and controlled manner, it can be of use.

It must be mentioned here that repoussé, embossing, chasing and engraving are all methods of working sheet metal, but the tools and techniques are different. The terms tend to be used rather loosely, so in order to avoid confusion, these will be discussed separately.

All the relief jewellery used to illustrate this section has been produced using sheet pewter, .175 mm (.007 in) thick, mounted on aluminium and steel findings (figure 51). Though possessing considerable strength, the metal is very thin and can easily be cut with scissors. It is also very easily scratched and bent, so take care when cutting it. Once the surface has been damaged the marks are impossible to eradicate, so it is a good policy to store the sheets wrapped round smooth cardboard.

The pewter is modelled both from the wrong side and from the right side, the metal being pressed and coaxed into relief. Owing to the composition of the alloy, no work hardening takes place, therefore annealing is not necessary. However, the pewter requires support whilst pressure is being applied. Care must be taken to work on a base sufficiently resilient to allow the shaping of the metal. A piece of lino is ideal and forms a firm, yet springy base. Greater resiliency can be achieved by placing a piece of soft cloth between the pewter and the lino.

Handling the tools

The tools for relief modelling consist of a straight tracer, a bent tracer, a modeller, a double-ended ball tool and a retractable ball-point pen, devoid of ink (figure 44).

Before starting to model an actual design, it is advisable to practise with the tools on a scrap of pewter, so that one becomes accustomed to the variety of effects which can be achieved and to the amount of pressure required to obtain these effects (figure 45). With a little practice, lines,

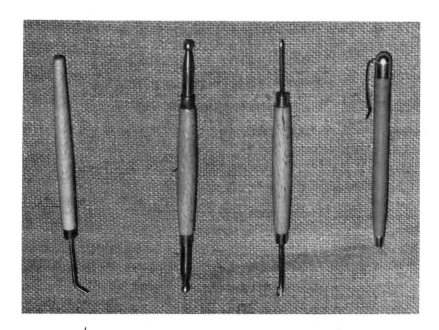

Figure 44 : Tools used for modelling in relief (left to right) : bent tracer, ball punch, straight tracer and modeller, an old ball-point pen case

Figure 45 : Some suggestions for making practice strokes

shapes and eventually an all-over pattern can be worked, which can probably be utilized in some way (figure 46), so that the practice metal is not wasted.

The straight tracer is held in the right hand, like a pencil and is used for tracing and pricking outlines. It can also be used for making fine lines on both sides of the work and for producing a pinprick background.

The bent tracer is held in the right hand, steadied with the left hand and worked, space permitting, from left to right. It is used for impressing the outline on both sides of the work, the smoothness of the tool giving a well defined edge to the design. It is also useful when setting stones into sheet pewter (figures 47, 48).

Figure 46 : A practice piece put to good use

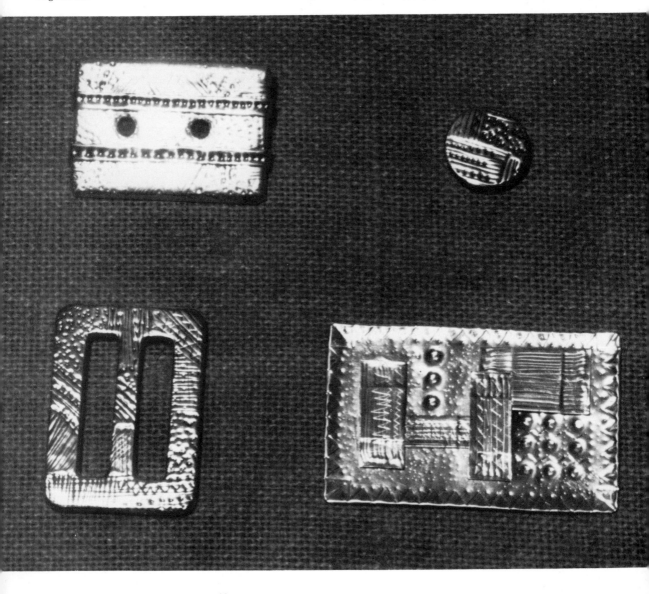

42

Figure 47 : When using the bent tracer try to work from left to right

Figure 48 : The bent tracer is held in the right hand and steadied with the left hand

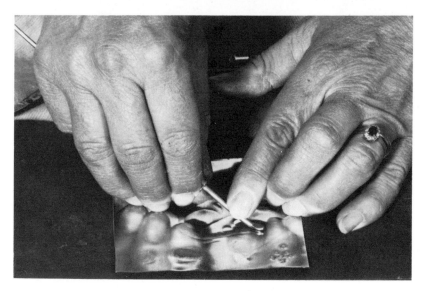
Figure 49 : The modeller is held in the right hand and steadied with the left hand – a swinging action is used to help raise areas of the design

43

The modeller is used to raise areas of the design. A smooth swinging action is used, the tool once again being held in the right hand and steadied with the left hand. It can also be used successfully to impress a line when there is insufficient room for the bent tracer, but the definition is not as crisp as when using the bent tracer (figure 49).

The double-ended ball punch is used upright, like a stencilling brush, to impress hollows. When held upright using a circular motion, an interesting swirling effect is obtained. The neck of the tool is invaluable when mounting finished work onto findings.

The retractable ball-point pen, when held like the punch, makes a perfect circle. When held like the straight tracer, it helps to give definition to outlines and can be used successfully for putting in detailed markings.

Using the tools mentioned, interesting backgrounds can be achieved (figure 50). By introducing objects like an old crab's claw, or a piece of rounded knitting needle, a greater variety of markings can be obtained.

Figure 50 : Different background textures :
(top left) the ball-point pen with the point retracted;
(top right) the claw from a crab;
(bottom left) the straight tracer and ball-point pen;
(bottom right) the punch

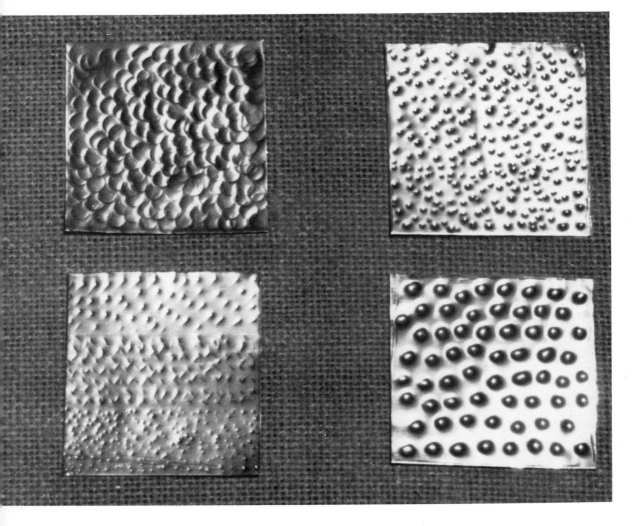

Using Findings

The term 'finding' refers to the basic metal shapes, known as blanks, upon which other metals and gems can be mounted (figure 51), as well as to the links and attachments used for fixing and fastening jewellery (figure 52). Jump rings can be used to attach pendants to necklace chains or leather thongs, or to connect one section of a bracelet to another. They can be opened and closed easily with small round-nosed pliers. Bell caps can be glued to the top of pendants, such as stones or chunky pieces, through which it is not possible or desirable to pierce a hole to take the jump ring. Earring findings can take the form of ear wires, loops with screws, or posts with butterfly attachments for pierced ears, while earclips, which come in many different shapes, are used for non-pierced ears.

Links and chains can be bought, or made by winding wire round a circular rod, removing the rod, and cutting through the spiral with metal snips. If a ring is found to be too large for the finger, a ring clip

Figure 51 : A selection of aluminium and steel findings, or blanks

45

Figure 52 : Findings, or fastenings, for necklaces, earrings, brooches and cuff links: (a) bell cap, (b) jump ring, (c) bolt ring, (d) spring catch, (e) ear wire, (f) ear screw and loop, (g) ear post and butterfly, (h) spring earclip, (i) bar pin, (j) safety chain, (k) ring clip, (l) chain cuff link, (m) swivel cuff link

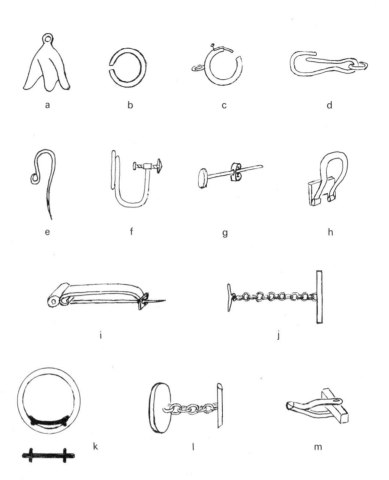

may be positioned inside it to make the inner circumference smaller. Most ring blanks used for pewter jewellery are open on the underside of the ring and therefore easily adjustable.

A wide range of jewellery can be made if full advantage is taken of all the findings available. Pendants and brooch blanks of varying shapes and sizes, bracelets and bangles, rings, tiepins and cufflinks are all obtainable, as are plain aluminium discs of different shapes. Plain buttons and buckles can be made more interesting and individual by covering them with pewter (figure 46).

The same methods of working and finishing are used throughout, only the mounting differs according to the finding. Great care is necessary when mounting bangles to prevent the pewter from creasing (figure 62).

It is preferable to use an impact adhesive (such as Evostik, UHU, or DuPont's Duco Cement) for gluing worked pewter onto the finding. These glues produce an excellent adhesion providing the manufacturer's instructions are followed.

Where only one side of the finding is to be covered with pewter (for example, brooches, bangles and buttons) it is advisable, when trimming away the surplus metal, to trim to within 3 mm (just over $\frac{1}{8}$ in), thus giving a slightly wider lap over. Any corners must be cut away to facilitate easy turning (figure 53). Brooches can then be backed with leather to prevent any possibility of the metal soiling lightly-coloured clothing.

In the case of rings, earrings and bracelets, no turnings are allowed. The metal is cut away level with the finding, pressed into position and smoothed with emery paper. Plain discs and aluminium shapes, which are going to be attached to earclips, leather, or some other material, are trimmed in the same way.

Figure 53 : The reverse side of an octagonal brooch, with the corners cut, ready for turning

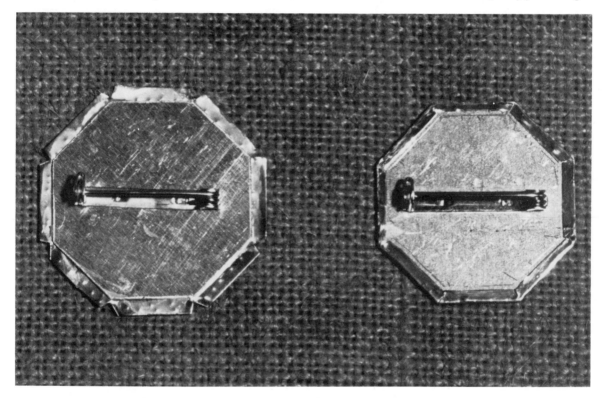

Modelling a Pendant

Materials and Equipment

sheet pewter	straight tracer
pendant finding	bent tracer
resilient work base	modeller
filler	ball punch
grease remover	retractable ball-point pen
pewter patina	curved scissors
cotton wool (cotton swab)	tracing paper
adhesive	old toothbrush
emery paper No 600	old knife
lacquer (optional)	pencil

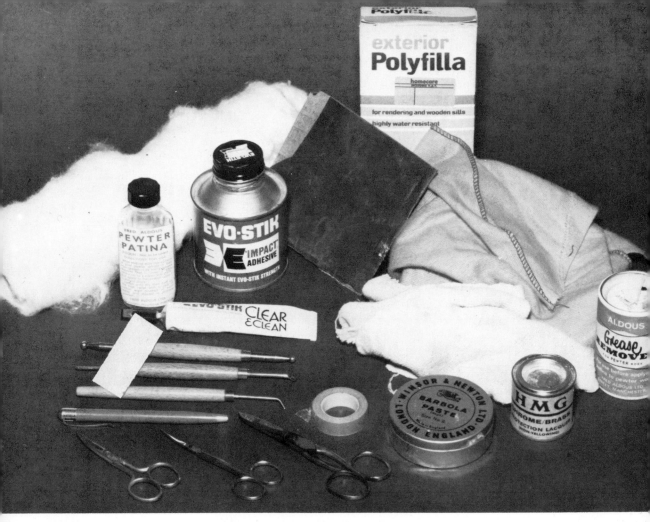

Figure 54 : Equipment for modelling in relief

Stage 1 : Transferring the design to the metal

Cut two pieces of pewter 12 mm ($\frac{1}{2}$ in) larger than the finding. Draw or trace the design onto tracing paper. Place this over one piece of pewter and secure them both onto the lino base with an adhesive strip of tape. Using the straight tracer, draw the main lines of the design, omitting all detail at this stage (figure 55).

It must be remembered that this is the wrong side of the work, so the design is in reverse. If the outline of the finding is marked at this stage it simplifies the mounting process later.

Stage 2 : Tooling the work

Place a layer of soft cloth, such as a duster, between the lino and the pewter. Using the bent tracer, impress the line made by the straight tracer, thus raising the design on the right side. Now with the right side uppermost, repeat this process, working just outside the raised areas, to give definition to the shape (figure 56).

Turn the work once more so that the wrong side is uppermost, making sure that the work surface is resilient enough to allow the metal to be raised yet further with the modeller and the ball punch. At this stage, having created the outline in relief, it is advisable to work from the

48

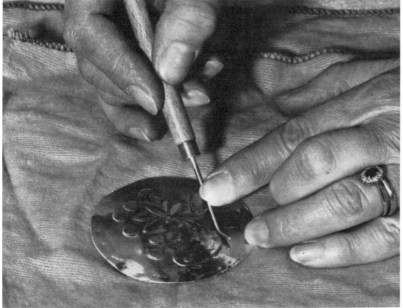

middle of the design, raising the larger areas first, before adding any detail from either side.

When the desired effect has been achieved, the duster can be removed and with the pewter resting directly on the lino, right side uppermost, the background is first pressed flat with the fingers, before giving a final definition to the outlines of the design. The textured background adds a finishing touch. The second piece of pewter is tooled in the same way.

Stage 3 : Filling

Remembering the malleability of the metal, it is essential that the raised areas of the jewellery are strengthened to prevent dinting and damage whilst it is being worn. This is done by using a plaster or a paste on the reverse side of the work. There are a number of reputable products on the market suitable for this purpose (such as Wallart, Plaster of Paris Powder, Polycel or Barbola Paste). Provided that they are used according to the manufacturers' instructions, they will give satisfactory results.

An old knife is admirable for smoothing the filler into position (figure 57). When using any of the above mentioned products on a bangle which has to be mounted on a highly sprung steel finding, it is advisable to establish the curve before filling. This helps to reduce cracking as the filler dries.

Figure 57 : Infilling the raised areas of the design

Stage 4 : Cleaning

Grease remover, which is similar to pumice powder and is obtainable from craft shops and jeweller's suppliers, is recommended for removing all traces of finger marks and dirt. Dampen a soft cloth or a piece of cotton wool with cold water, sprinkle with the powder and rub until all the black residue has been removed. Wash with cold water and dry the metal, taking care not to dampen the filling. A final polish with a soft cloth will produce a high lustrous finish and the pewter can be left in this state. However, if desired, it can be darkened artificially.

Stage 5 : Oxidizing

This is a method of artificially darkening the pewter to give it an antique appearance. A preparation sold as pewter patina is used for this purpose. It should be evenly applied with a piece of cotton wool (cotton swab) over the entire surface and allowed to dry (figure 58). If the metal was totally immersed, the filling would be affected.

As soon as the pewter comes into contact with the patina it immediately turns black, showing slight traces of blue residue. These oxides are wiped away and the cleaning process is repeated, using more grease remover and a damp cloth. This results in a most attractive surface, as the areas of relief are highlighted and the lower areas remain dark, depending upon the intensity of the polishing.

Figure 58 : Applying patina with a pad of cotton wool

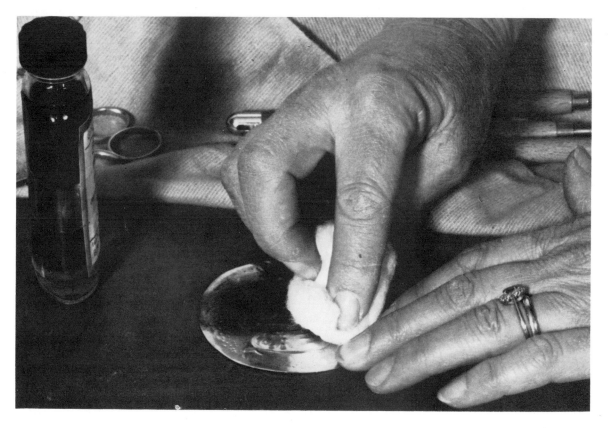

Stage 6 : Mounting the pendant

Prepare both pieces of pendant by snipping a small 'V' to enable the work to fit snugly round the jump ring.

Glue the piece of pewter destined to be the reverse side of the pendant into position first. When the glue is almost set, with curved scissors trim the surplus pewter away to within 2 mm ($\frac{1}{12}$ in) of the finding (figure 59).

Figure 59: Using curved scissors to trim away the excess pewter

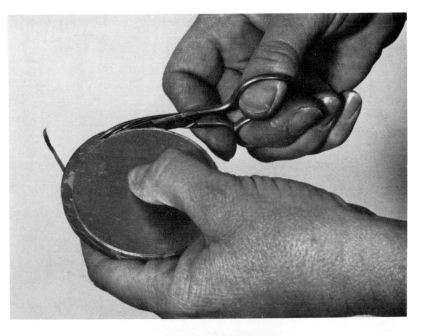

Figure 60: Using the neck of the ball tool to press down the edge of the pewter

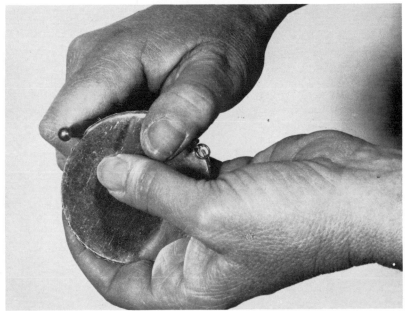

52

Using the neck of the ball tool, press the edge of the pewter down firmly. Smooth with emery paper if necessary. Mount the remaining piece of pewter in the same way, but leave slightly more pewter when trimming the edge 2.5 mm ($\frac{1}{10}$ in). Press this firmly down and finish as for the reverse side (figure 60). The finding should now be completely covered with pewter and the pendant can be coated with lacquer if desired (figure 61).

Figure 61 : The completed pendant

Modelling a Matching Set of Jewellery

Trace the designs given in figures 62, 63, 64 and 65, and transfer them onto sheet pewter .175 mm (.007 in) thick. Model the designs in relief, then mount the pewter on bangle and brooch blanks following the methods given above. The smaller designs are suitable for rings, or may be combined to form the components of a sectioned bracelet to match.

Gold leaf or polyurethane paint may also be used to give colour to the unraised parts of a design. Gold leaf is available in booklet form, each sheet backed by tissue, and should be handled carefully. (A safe way of picking it up is with a brush rather than with the fingers – run the brush over your hair to create static electricity and the sheet of gold leaf will be easily picked up and transferred to the metal on the end of the brush.) First coat the surface to be gilded with gold size (or 101 polyurethane yellow paint), allow this to become tacky, then lay the gold leaf face down onto the painted surface (with the tissue still adhering to the back). Pad it down carefully with a stiff bristle brush, and leave for about 12 hours until dry, then dust off any untidy specks of gold with a soft brush.

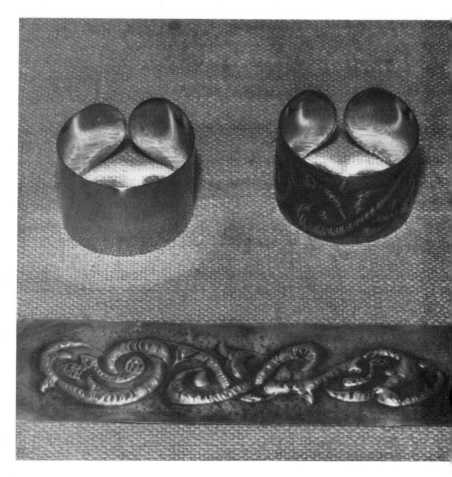

Figure 62a : Design for a bangle

Figure 62b : The bangle before and after mounting

Figure 63a : Designs for gold leaf inlay

Figure 63b : A matching set with gold leaf inlay

Figure 64 : Designs using a
Viking theme

Figure 65 : Ideas which could be used for earrings or buttons

Setting Stones

The most suitable stones to choose for this type of work are cabochons, which are usually round or oval with a flat base and a domed upper surface. They are cut to exact sizes, so that holes can be prepared accurately.

If transparent stones are chosen, the backs must be covered with either tissue paper or tinfoil so that any glue marks will not be visible. Most lapidary dealers can also supply other ranges of flat-backed stones, such as shell cameos, zodiac stones and others which would be enhanced by a pewter surround.

To help with the preparation of the holes, a pair of compasses and a leather punch are useful, though not essential.

There are two methods of setting the stones. Using the first method, the stones are set into the worked pewter, before infilling has taken place, and then they are both mounted together onto the finding. In the second method, the stones are fixed onto the findings and the pewter is then mounted over them.

First method

Mark the position of the stone or stones clearly on the drawing and then the piece of worked pewter (figure 66a). The size of the hole should be 2 mm ($\frac{1}{12}$ in) less in diameter than the stone. This allows for a collet (a projecting flat rim or collar) which is both decorative and useful for keeping the stone in position.

Cut across the circle of pewter to be removed so that the lines intersect and divide the waste metal into quarters (figure 66b).

Test the hole for size by placing the stone on a flat surface and start to gently stretch and ease the pewter into position, with the help of the bent tracer (figure 66c). When satisfied, cut away the surplus pewter and file away any rough edges (figure 66d). Oval stones can be fitted in the same way.

57

Figure 66 :

(a) Mark the position of the stone

(b) Cut the pewter outwards from the centre in four directions

(c) Ease the stone and pewter into position

(d) The surplus metal can then be removed

Another method of cutting a hole for a circular stone is to use a pair of compasses. Having located the position of the stone, the sharp point of the compasses is used to inscribe the circle with ever increasing pressure, until the piece of pewter is removed.

Cutting a small hole can be a problem, but if 7 mm ($\frac{1}{4}$ in) or 8 mm ($\frac{3}{8}$ in) circular stones are to be used, the largest hole on a leather punch is ideal for punching the holes. Cut these from the wrong side, so that the raised edge appears on the right side of the work. This will form the collet. It is always advisable to test for size on a scrap of pewter first.

Having cut the hole, the collet is raised by placing the bent end of the modelling tool underneath the cut edge and rotating the pewter slowly, applying the same amount of pressure all the time (figure 67). If the stretching is gradual and the hole frequently checked for size, a good fit will be obtained. Once again, smooth any rough areas with emery paper.

When the holes have been prepared, using a colourless adhesive, glue carefully round the collet and drop the stones into position from the wrong side of the work. To secure the back, stick a piece of tissue paper over the stone, so that it slightly overlaps the surrounding pewter.

To ensure a snug, tidy fit, the collet is pressed into position with the bent tracer (figure 68), and burnished with the smooth side of the modeller to give a finished appearance. The work is then ready for mounting in the usual way.

58

Figure 67 : Raising the collet with the help of the modelling tool

Figure 68 : Pressing the collet into position with the bent tracer

Second method

In jewellery making, this method is not to be recommended except when making a ring. Cut the pewter to size, mark the position of the stone, and cut out the hole. Glue the stone onto the finding. It might be necessary to roughen the base of the stone, so that it grips firmly. Then lay the pewter over the top, and smooth it into position.

Designs with Set-in Stones

When using stones on a bangle, although they are set into the pewter whilst it is still flat, it is advisable not to choose very large stones. Oval stones should be positioned vertically and not horizontally (figure 69).

As with most crafts, there must always be room for further experimentation (figure 70). Separate collets of varying designs, shaped and cut to measure the circumference of the stone to be set, could be fashioned and glued or soldered into position. Holes can be cut out of findings, and faceted stones can be set held in position by claws or bell caps. Always look for variation in techniques.

Trace the following designs (figures 71 to 78) and use them to make matching sets with set-in stones.

Figure 69 : Bangles showing round and oval stones

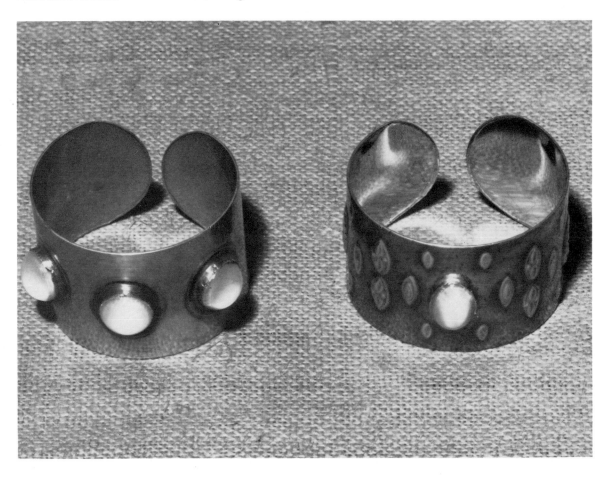

Figure 70 : 7 mm ($\frac{1}{4}$ in) stones set into the fish, mounted on leather

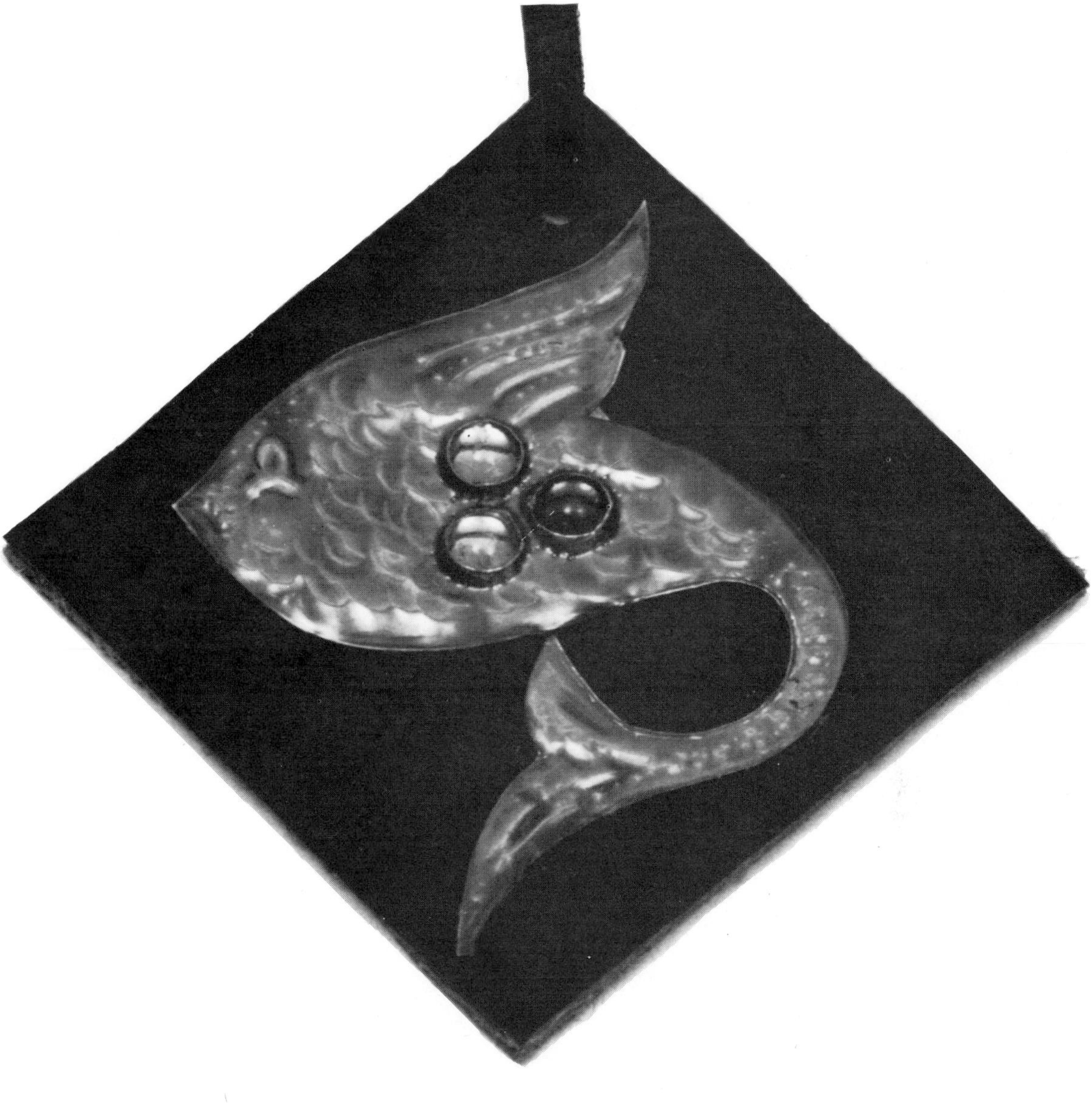

Figure 71 : Diagram for a cameo pendant and brooch

Figure 72 : The worked cameo pendant

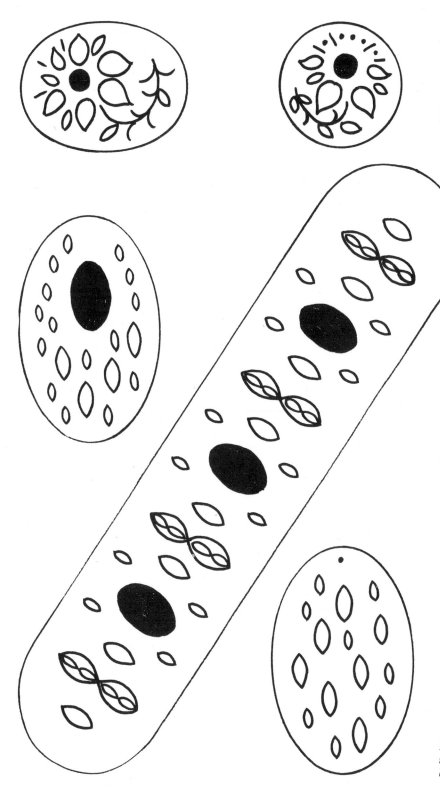

Figure 73 : (far left) Design for an oval brooch with a 7 mm ($\frac{1}{4}$ in) stone

Figure 74 : (left) Design for a round brooch with a 7 mm ($\frac{1}{4}$ in) stone

Figure 75 : Designs for a matching bangle, pendant and brooch, using oval cabochons

63

Figure 76 : Design for a bangle
using masks

64

Figure 77 : Design for a bangle using flowers and small stones

Figure 78 : Cabochons set into pewter bangles, pendants, brooches and rings, modelled in relief

65

Advanced Modelling Techniques

Repoussé, Chasing and Embossing

Repoussé, chasing and embossing are all methods of modelling sheet metal in relief. Repoussé (from the French verb *pousser* 'to push') is the technique of modelling sheet metal from the reverse side, whilst the technique of defining areas of ornamentation, and adding fine lines and precise details from the right side, is called chasing. Embossing is raising or stamping the metal from the wrong side. No doubt the word 'boss', the central stud of a shield, derives from the same root.

Objects, often of silver, where chasing alone has been used are quite common. On highly decorative articles, where the metal requires raising, it is difficult to use one technique without the other. Yet specimens of pewter jewellery using these well established methods of decoration are rare.

The tools of the craft can boast a long history. The work, requiring much skill, is done entirely with punches and hammers, so obviously the metal is subjected to a considerable amount of pressure and strain. Nevertheless, owing to the malleability of pewter, it will allow itself to be stretched and beaten without work hardening and without cracking. However, the soft velvety surface of the metal will soon dint and damage if it is not correctly supported whilst it is being worked.

Jeweller's suppliers offer pitch bowls, pitch boards and engraver's sandbags for this purpose. If using a pitch bowl, onto which the metal is placed face downwards, it must be remembered to keep the pitch warm and pliable whilst it is being worked. This is a messy, dirty process, but gives excellent detail and accurate definition. In the case of the amateur with a small piece of jewellery, other methods of supporting the work are worth considering, if quality can be sacrificed slightly in return for a cleaner method.

An engraver's sandbag, made of leather, approximately 150 mm (6 in) in diameter, dispenses with the inconvenience of a pitch bowl. It leaves both hands free to operate the tools and provide a base of the correct resilience, but it is not cheap.

A sufficiently padded wooden block provides an alternative satisfactory working surface, as long as the resiliency of the base permits the pewter to be raised to the required height.

The punches are easily recognizable. Generally speaking, repoussé

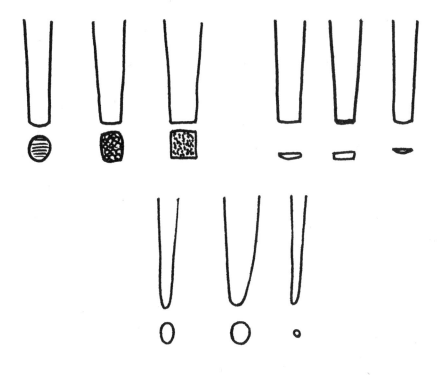

Figure 79 : Repoussé, chasing and texturing punches

punches are rounded, possessing no sharp edges, thus enabling areas to be raised smoothly. Chasing punches, however, have sharper edges, to enable more defined lines to be hammered from the right side of the work. Texturing and matting punches, each with a different pattern imprinted on the end, enable interesting backgrounds to be worked (figure 79). A degree of skill must be achieved before attempting a set piece of jewellery. The aim is to keep the punch moving evenly across the surface of the work, as it is being hammered, so that the thickness of the metal remains the same.

While the pewter is being supported, the main areas of the design are transferred with a grease pencil or a tracing tool onto the reverse side of the article. Tooling of the work commences with the raising of the larger areas first to the required height. All detail of the design is transferred after defining these areas. During the working, the metal is frequently changed from wrong to right side and vice versa, until the appearance is satisfactory. Remember that the background should always be in lower relief and never allowed to dominate the design.

When the required amount of decoration and detail has been achieved, infilling must take place to support and protect the raised areas, before degreasing and a final cleaning.

Engraving

The craft of engraving is highly skilled, and a person wishing to master this technique first needs to be shown by an expert, and then needs to practise and practise. It is not a skill that can be learnt in a hurry.

67

The decoration, worked entirely on the right side, is done with tools known as gravers and scorpers (figure 80), the points of which are pushed along just below the surface of the metal. Pewter, being a soft metal, is easy to engrave, but the danger is that too much metal can be removed. Much less pressure has to be applied than when engraving on silver.

The work is positioned on an engraver's sandbag (figure 81) and balanced with the left hand. Many engravers shorten the shaft of their tools from the handle end, so that they fit the palm of the hand exactly and are comfortable to use.

The pendant shown (figure 82) was engraved using a square graver, a half round, a flat scorper and a thread tool, or a multiple liner.

Figure 80 : An engraver's scorper

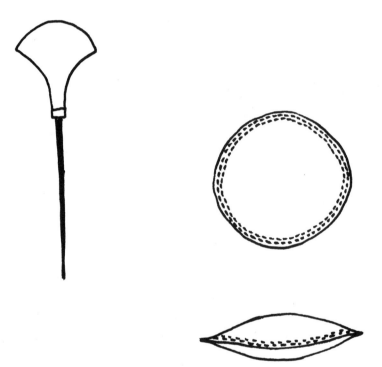

Figure 81 : (far right) An engraver's sandbag

Figure 82 : (opposite page) Pendant cast by Nigel Edmondson, engraved by Sue Blackman, American ex-student of the Sir John Cass School of Art, London

Hammering

A tremendous variety of attractive finishes, ranging from random circular indentations to linear patterns, can be produced on sheet metal by hammering. The metal must be supported on a firm base, such as a lead or wooden block, before pressure is applied.

Short, sharp, swift blows with a hammer, the head of which has been scored to give a textured effect, can be used to advantage. Punches, nail heads and other workshop tools can be used in conjunction with a hammer to produce more varied results (figures 83, 84, 85).

Figure 83: This eleven-piece necklace by Nigel Edmondson was made from pierced and hammered pewter sheet

Figure 84: A hammered pewter brooch, found in a junk shop

Casting

Casting, the technique of pouring molten metal into a mould and allowing it to solidify to produce a single article, was in use before 2000 BC.

Early man cast implements and most probably body ornaments in moulds of stone, clay and sand. Modern man, whilst still using simple methods of casting in some circumstances, has also evolved more sophisticated and costly methods to produce moulds which cast either a single replica of a design, or accurate repetitions of one pattern, depending upon the chosen method and the equipment used.

The suitability of pewter as a metal for casting has already been discussed. Its melting point of between 218.3°C and 226.6°C (425°F and 440°F), when compared with that of copper, silver and gold, is very much in its favour. (A table of melting points is supplied at the end of the book.)

It is, nevertheless, vitally important to remember that, whether one is using a simple method of casting or a more complicated method, a successful cast cannot be made without a carefully prepared mould.

Pewter, for use when casting, can either be bought from dealers as scrap and melted down into manageable pieces or it can be obtained as specially prepared slabs and ingots. The latter form is more costly.

Owing to the objectionable fumes produced when melting down scrap, it is advisable to carry out this operation in a well ventilated space. The debris present in the metal will float to the top and can easily be scooped off with a spoon before the molten metal is poured into small cans. Any spare metal left over from sheet pewter used for relief work can also be used for casting. The pieces of jewellery shown in this section have all been made out of recycled pewter.

Casting with Cuttlefish Bone

Materials and equipment

cuttlefish bone
saw
emery papers No 120, 240, 360, 600
variety of modelling tools for
    drawing, scraping and impressing
stiff brush No 4 bristle
binding wire
ladle and stand
adequate heat (gas ring, or torch and
    calor gas cylinder)

fire brick (or similar object) to steady
    the mould
wire brush
assorted files
patina
pewter
charcoal block
snips and pliers
drill
adhesive for fixing stones

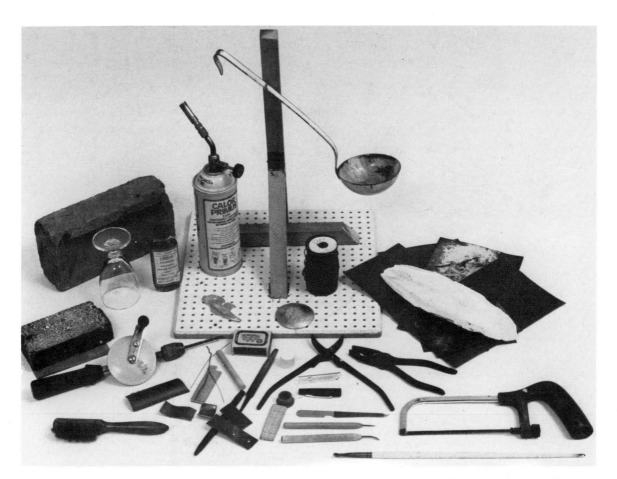

Figure 86 : Equipment for casting, using cuttlefish bone

Practically all the equipment, apart from the bone and the pewter, can either be found in the home workshop, or made very easily. The tool for drawing the outline can be made from a large needle set into a piece of dowelling. Similarly, the tool for scraping the bone can be made from a flattened nail set into a handle. The modelling tools consist of pieces of wood with shaped ends, bits of metal, glass and plastic tubing, and oddments of pewter.

Before starting to prepare the mould, it is advisable to give some thought to the type of design which will cast successfully. Making a model in plasticine, prior to carving in the bone, helps to give an idea of the finished product. It is vital to remember the following points.

(1) The pieces of bone which are removed will form the shape of the cast.
(2) The pieces of bone which remain after carving will appear as holes in the completed piece of jewellery.
(3) The design is carved in reverse.
(4) If the carving is shallow, the piece of jewellery will be quite light.
(5) If the carving is deep and extensive, the resulting piece of jewellery will be fairly heavy.

73

Preparing the bone

Cuttlefish bone, the internal bone of the cuttlefish, can be obtained from jeweller's suppliers or sometimes from pet shops. It weighs very little, so when ordering by post, only a small quantity, 1 kg (2 lb), would be ample and would provide sufficient bones for experimentation. The outer shell is extremely hard in contrast to the centre, which is soft and inclined to crumble. The pointed ends are usually removed with a saw and only the thicker middle portions are used for carving (figure 87, 88).

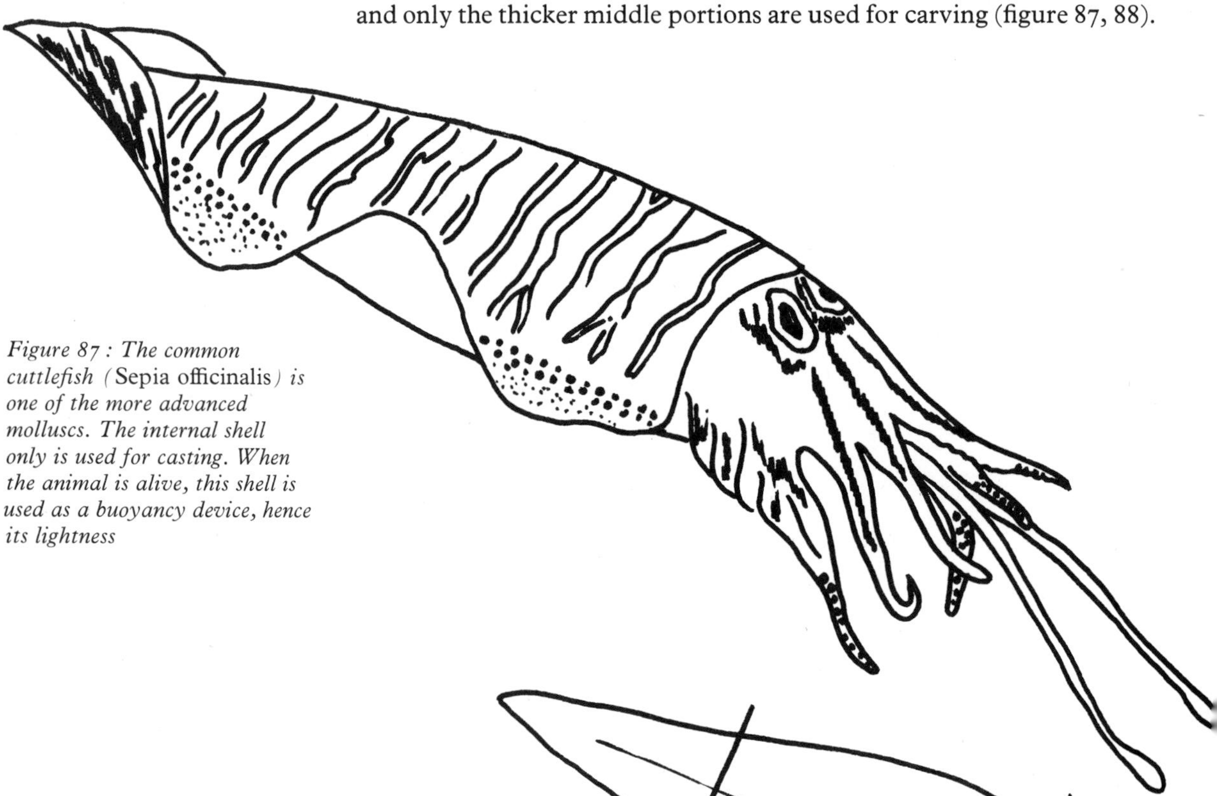

*Figure 87 : The common cuttlefish (*Sepia officinalis*) is one of the more advanced molluscs. The internal shell only is used for casting. When the animal is alive, this shell is used as a buoyancy device, hence its lightness*

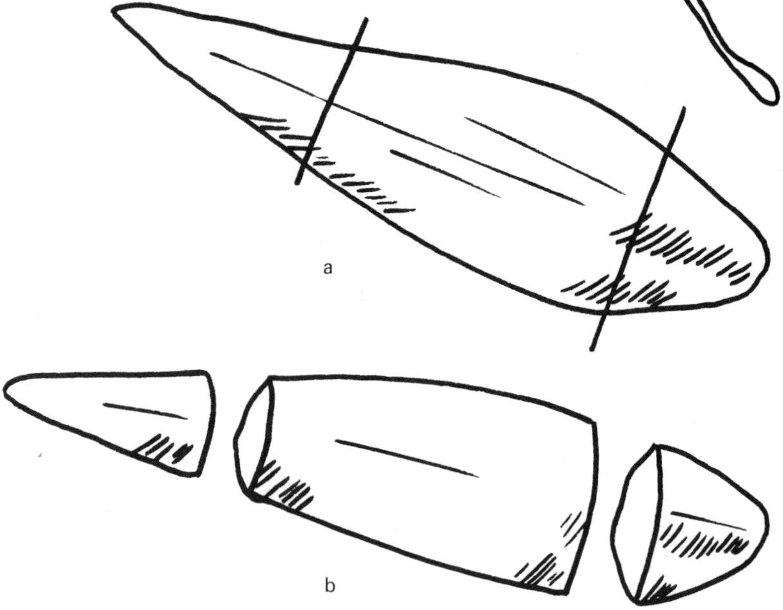

a

Figure 88 :
(a) The ends of the shell are removed with a saw

(b) Only the centre section is used

b

Casting a Pendant

The design used for the pendant worked in relief has been adapted here for casting.

(1) Rub the softer side of the bone level and smooth using coarse emery paper No 120 (figure 89).

(2) Snip away the hard outer edges of the shell to enable the bone to be faced up to a charcoal block (figure 90).

(3) Face the bone up to the charcoal block by rubbing the two sides

Figure 89 : Levelling the soft side of the bone on coarse emery paper

Figure 90 : Removing the hard outer edge of the shell

together until a film of grey powder covers the bone. This shows that the two sides will be in close contact when casting (figure 91).

(4) The bone is now ready for carving. Depending upon the design chosen, this can either be done free-hand, or shapes can be used to impress the pattern. A gate must be carved through which the pewter will enter the mould. It is advisable to scratch air vents through which any accumulated air can escape (figure 92).

(5) To reveal the grain of the cuttlefish bone, remove the dust carefully

Figure 91 : Facing up the bone to the charcoal block

Figure 92 : The curved mould, showing the gate through which the molten pewter will enter the mould, and the air vents through which accumulated air can escape

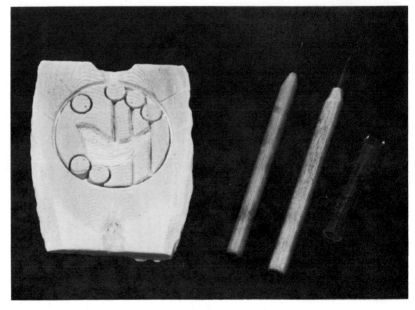

with a small bristle brush. It is essential to remove any bits of crumbled bone which might impede the flow of the molten pewter (figure 93). (6) Bind the mould and charcoal block together with fine wire. If the block has a pitted surface, insert a piece of hardboard between the bone and the block, with the smooth side of the board to the bone. (7) Place the pewter in a ladle and heat it either over a gas ring or by directing a naked flame onto the metal. Remove any impurities which will float to the top with an old spoon (figure 94).

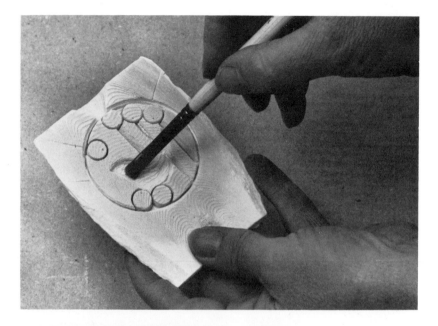

Figure 93 : Cleaning the mould with a bristle brush, to ensure that dust and all fine particles of bone are removed

Figure 94 : Melting the pewter by playing a flame directly onto the metal – it can also be melted over a gas ring

(8) Pour the metal into the mould and allow it to solidify and cool for between 10 and 15 minutes (figure 95).

(9) Lift the pendant out of the mould and remove the gate with a saw or snips. If an electric polisher is not available, the pendant can be hand-polished using the coarse emery paper first and gradually working down to the finer grades. Small bits of metal can easily be removed with metal files of varying sizes and shapes (figure 96).

(10) If an antique finish is required, immerse the pendant in the patina and wash off the surplus liquid with cold water.

(11) Clean with a wire brush or an old toothbrush, before giving the pendant a final polish with fine emery paper to highlight the metal.

(12) If the completed pendant requires drilling to receive a jump ring or leather thong, it is advisable to mark the position of the hole with a punch, to prevent the drill from wandering off course. In the case of the pendant shown here, a hole was cast in the design.

Figure 95 : Pouring the molten metal. Note that the cuttlefish has been faced up to hardboard and the charcoal block. This helps when the charcoal is becoming pitted and uneven

Figure 96 : The cast pendant before removing from the mould, and the same pendant after removing the gate, polishing and treating it with patina

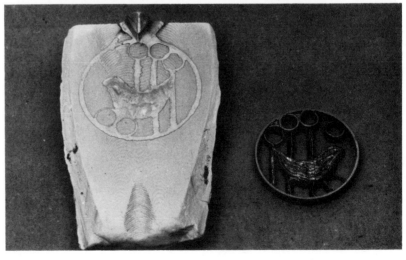

Casting Complex Shapes

Casting a button

To cast an article such as a decorative button, it is necessary to produce a button head and a shank. To cast them separately could produce soldering problems, but to cast the button in one piece is a relatively simple procedure.

In this case the charcoal block was dispensed with, and one piece of cuttlefish was divided in two. A central spot was marked on each piece of bone. The button head was carved in one piece and an indentation was made for the shank in the other piece of bone. Care was taken to locate the centres before binding the two pieces together. This can be done by marking the outer shell. This method is quite successful, and the mould used in the example was still intact after three castings (figure 97). A hole for the thread is then drilled through the shank.

Figure 97 : The mould in two parts, and the cast buttons

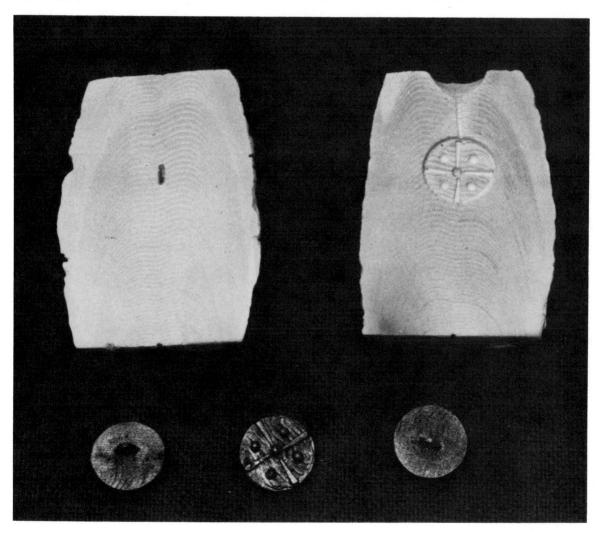

Casting a random line design

Two pieces of bone were also used to cast the adaptation of the fish design (figure 38). Here, the punch illustrated in the relief work chapter was used to form a series of indentations into the bone, which were joined by lines scratched with the straight tracer. Using the punch in this way suggests a number of different ideas (figures 98, 99).

Figure 98 : Diagrams showing adaptations of designs shown earlier in the book, using the punch and line idea

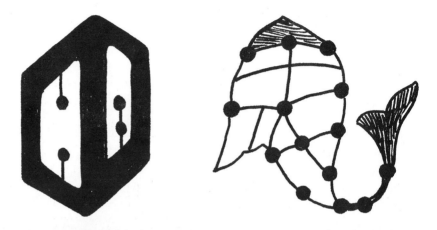

Figure 99 : A pendant and brooch (punch and line)

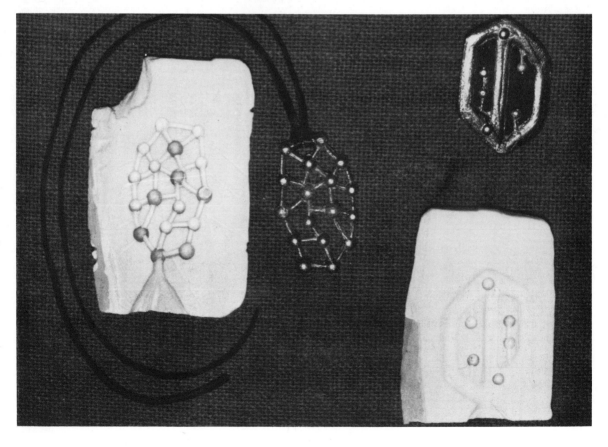

Casting a bracelet and matching pendant

Before casting the components for the bracelet and the matching pendant, prepare the moulds in the following manner. Mark and scrape away the oblong outline shapes to a depth of approximately 3 mm ($\frac{1}{10}$ in). Smooth the area carefully with a piece of pewter. Then use a plastic pen top to impress the circles (figure 100).

Figure 100 : Pendant and bracelet, showing the moulds. The smaller mould was particularly good, and was used four times in all

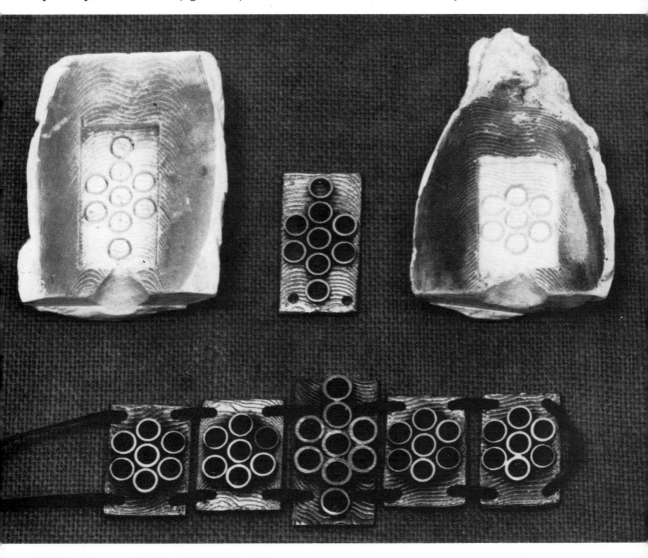

Setting Stones in Cuttlefish Moulds

The easiest stones to set are cabochons, but when embedding a stone, the shape can be more adventurous.

When setting a stone, the most important point to remember is that the girdle, the widest part of the stone, is supported by means of a base, or a bezel. This allows the stone to sit correctly, perfectly balanced, before the collet (the metal surrounding the stone), which can be plain or

81

ornamental, is pushed into place. Three of the methods described here use a base and a collet.

A bezel is made by soldering a separate piece of metal round the inside edge of a collet to form a ledge upon which the stone can sit. This is not a simple process, and is not necessary when casting with cuttlefish.

Stones can be set by the following four methods:

(1)   Embedding the stone in the mould before casting
(2)   Casting a base and collet in which to set the stone
(3)   Casting a claw setting
(4)   Casting a base and a surround of shapes

Embedding the stone before casting

Some stones do disintegrate under heat, for example, some qualities of opals, so it is better to choose a stone which shows no obvious lines along which it might crack.

(1) Draw and scrape out the shape of the jewellery.
(2) Locate the position and scrape out the indentation made by the stone.

Figure 101 : Mould and pendant showing an embedded stone, a blue snowflake obsidian (courtesy Ron Cooper)

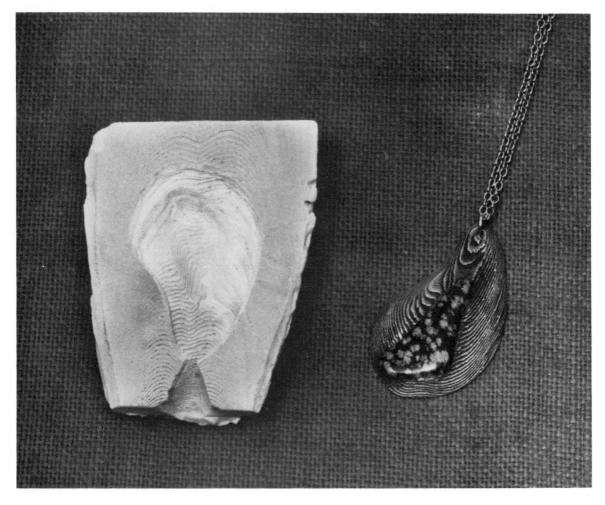

(3) With a spot of adhesive, lightly fix the stone, face downwards, into the indentation in the bone.

(4) Prepare and cast in the usual way.

(5) Carefully remove the bone and glue sticking to the stone.

(6) Finish in the normal way, but it is not advisable to immerse a stone in patina (figure 101).

Casting a base and collet

To cast a base and collet is a fairly easy matter. It simplifies the task if a tool can be found with a circumference measuring fractionally more than the stone to be set.

(1) Impress the design into the bone, taking care to join each shape.

(2) Slightly scrape away those shapes which will be receiving a stone to form a level base. The impression around the shape, when filled with metal, forms a collet, which in due course will surround the stone.

(3) Prepare and cast in the usual way.

(4) After filing and polishing, fix the stones with adhesive (figure 102).

Figure 102 : Mould and casting, set with bright red cabochons

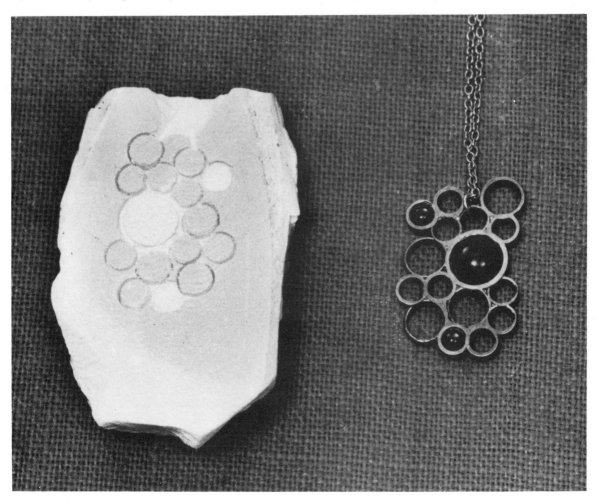

Casting a claw setting

(1) Mark the outline of the pendant and scrape away to a depth of 2 mm ($\frac{1}{12}$ in).

(2) Brush the grain of the bone to remove the dust.

(3) Using a fine tool, make impressions for the claws around the outline of the stone, in this case an abalone. (This is in reverse.)

(4) Prepare and cast in the usual way. Polish and patina the pendant.

(5) Although the claws will hold the stone, a spot of adhesive will act as an extra precaution.

(6) Snip the claws to the required length and taper them with a file from the outside. Then using a smooth steel tool, burnish them until they become bright, at the same time gradually coaxing them into position over the edge of the stone (figure 103).

Figure 103 : Mould and completed pendant showing an abalone in a claw setting

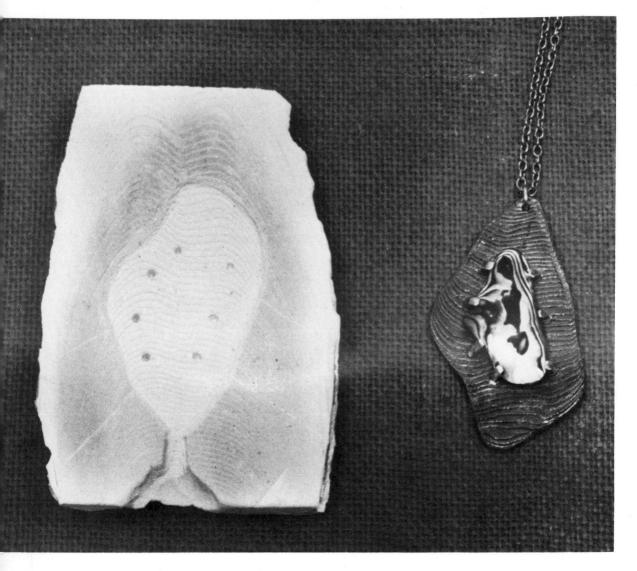

Casting a base and a surround of shapes

Follow the method given for casting a base and collet, substituting a tool which will provide the desired shapes (figure 104).

Correcting Faults

Difficulties do sometimes arise when casting with cuttlefish bone, and it is important to know how to correct them.

If the molten metal fails to remain in the mould, check points 1 and 2.
(1) Check that the bone has been faced up to the block or another piece of bone accurately. Molten pewter will find a way through the smallest gap.
(2) It is advisable to check the position of the carving on the bone. At

Figure 104: A cast hexagon pendant, showing a rough base ready to receive the stone (courtesy Mike Hylton)

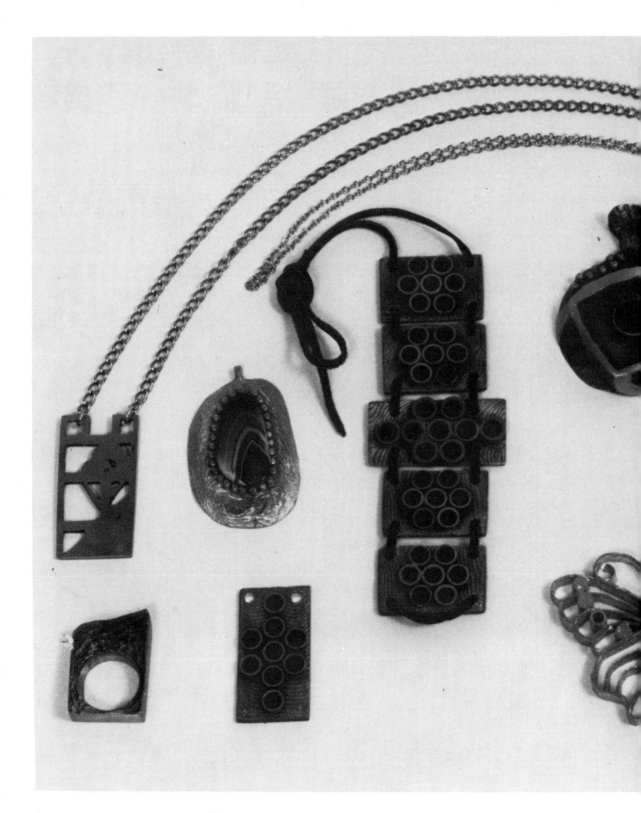

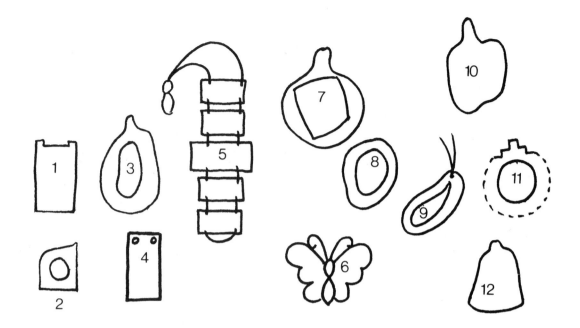

least 8 mm ($\frac{1}{4}$ in) clearance must be given between the design and the edge of the mould, more if the bone is large enough.

If the pewter fails to penetrate the entire mould, check points 3, 4 and 5.
(3) The molten pewter must enter the mould in one continuous pour, and on no account must it be allowed to cool before pouring.
(4) Make sure that the runways for the pewter are adequate. No line should be less than 2 mm ($\frac{1}{12}$ in) wide.
(5) Always melt a little more pewter than is required.

If an uneven piece of work is produced, check point 6.
(6) Try to use the same amount of pressure when impressing a design. It is preferable to press too far rather than not far enough. Excess pewter can always be filed away, but it cannot be added to the finished piece.

Sand Casting

Sand casting, one of the oldest techniques known to man, is still used today, especially to create chunky jewellery, where the surface of the article does not necessarily have to be perfectly smooth. Jean Pierre Massart, working in his studio in the south of France, interprets this method to perfection (figure 106).

When sandcasting, a model which has been carved in wood, hard wax or some other suitable material is used to make an impression in damp, fine silver sand, into which molten metal is poured.

First mix the sand, the finer the better, with a suitable binding material, such as white of egg, Isinglass or seaweed alginate to form a consistency similar to that needed to produce a successful sand castle!

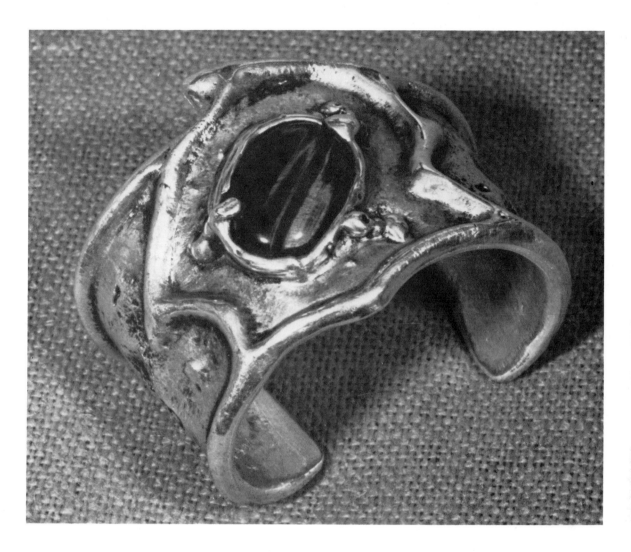

*Figure 106 : Cast pewter bangle
by Jean Pierre Massart*

(The sand must hold its shape.) It is then placed in a tray large enough to accommodate the object to be cast, the model of which is pressed into the damp sand to create an impression. It is advisable to leave a rim of sand around the model, not less than half its greatest diameter.

Molten metal is then poured into the impression and this will coagulate the binder and prevent the sand from crumbling, forming a crust round the casting. The top of such a casting will obviously be flat as in cuttlefish casting, and total reproduction of the surface can only be achieved by all round investment involving twin mating trays, with sprues to allow gas to escape. This is an extremely skilled process and beyond the scope of this book.

When the metal has set the crust can be broken away with a blunt probe, leaving the casting ready for 'fettling', a finished process carried out with hand stones and files to grind away the rough spicules. This method is only suitable for casting chunky objects requiring little detail.

89

Lost Wax Casting

Lost wax casting is a more complex technique. A wax model is made, which is placed inside a flask and completely surrounded by plaster. When the plaster has solidified, the wax is burnt out, leaving a cavity, into which the molten metal is poured. The plaster then has to be carefully broken to retrieve the cast. Moulds made in this manner are usually cast either by the Solbrig method, which relies upon steam and damp asbestos to force the molten metal into the flask, or by centrifugal casting, where part of the machine rotates at great speed, shooting the molten metal from a crucible into the flask. These machines are extremely costly, but are a necessity for the professional jeweller wishing to produce work to a very high standard.

So far all the methods of casting discussed have only produced a single cast. For mass production of jewellery, permanent, flexible moulds are made out of heat-resistant rubber. Numerous, identical wax patterns can be made from the same mould, invested and centrifugally cast, either singly or in groups. Once again, this is a costly process, designed for mass production manufacturing (figure 107).

Etching

The Basic Technique

Etching is the process whereby an acid is used to produce a recessed design on the right side of metal. Whereas copper can be etched rapidly, pewter takes longer for the acid to penetrate and bite away the metal. If a spot of nitric acid is dropped onto copper, a small circle of metal will quickly be eaten away, but in the case of pewter the reaction is less immediate. The chief component, tin, is less vulnerable to attack from acid.

First develop a design idea, then prepare a piece of sheet pewter. Shapes for making into pendants, earrings, or component pieces for bracelets can either be cast, or cut from the thicker grades of sheet pewter. During the preparation, ensure that all edges are smoothed, and that any holes required for jump rings, chains and thongs are drilled at this stage.

The chosen shape is then ready to be completely covered with an etching ground, which serves as a protection against the acid. A number of materials can be used for this purpose.

A stopping out varnish can be obtained from jeweller's suppliers, which can be painted directly onto the pewter. A more old fashioned method of making a ground is to use crushed sealing wax, dissolved in methylated spirit. Probably the easiest and most economical stopping out material to use is an ordinary household candle, which can be melted easily and applied with a thick, soft brush. The advantage of using candlewax is that it can be removed efficiently with hot water and soap.

Having chosen the etching ground and painted it onto the pewter, the problem now arises of transferring the design onto the ground, unless one is going to draw freehand.

Assuming that the design has been drawn on tracing paper, scribble very carefully over all the lines on the reverse side, and place this side down over the piece of metal. Very lightly (in order not to crack the wax) draw over the main lines, so that the pencil markings will transfer onto the ground.

Certain areas of wax must now be removed. If an etching needle is not available, the tip of a darning needle or a stiletto (used for broderie anglaise), or the extreme tip of the straight tracer used in relief work, are all suitable tools for the purpose.

Draw the design clearly, remembering that any metal exposed by the removal of the wax will be etched by the acid and will form part of the visible design. Care must be taken not to undercut the wax.

When the wax is quite firm, the piece of jewellery is then totally immersed in a mordant, that is, a solution of acid which forms an acid bath.

The mordant used for pewter consists of four parts of water to one part of nitric acid. When preparing the mordant, always POUR THE ACID INTO THE WATER. Do this in a well ventilated area to avoid inhaling the unpleasant fumes given off by the acid. A pyrex dish makes an excellent container. The mordant must be agitated from time to time, because if air bubbles are allowed to form and remain on the metal, the efficiency of the acid is impaired and the result will be uneven etching. This is done by stroking a feather across the surface to disperse any bubbles. The immersed article should be inspected from time to time and the metal scratched if etching appears to be slow. This speeds up the acid attack which appears at crystal boundaries and crevices in the alloy.

It is advisable to allow the etching to take place slowly because if too great a quantity of acid is used, it could probably generate sufficient heat to soften and lift the wax. When removing a piece of jewellery from the mordant, tongs must be used, so that it can be rinsed in cold water before being touched by hand. If the mordant does splash the skin, take the precaution of washing it off immediately with sodium bicarbonate.

When etching is complete, from 3 to 5 hours depending upon the depth of etch required, the jewellery can be finally removed from the mordant, rinsed with cold water and then brought into contact with hot water to remove the candlewax. If the wax is removed in a sink, keep the hot water running, as wax solidifies when cool and can easily block the drain.

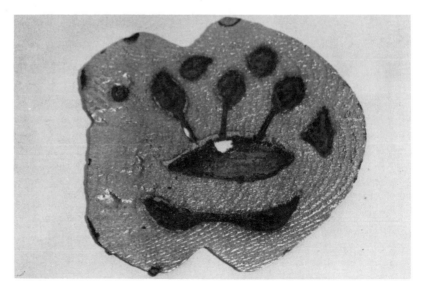

Figure 108 : Showing where the acid had eaten through the pewter

The experimental piece photographed was allowed to remain in the mordant for 7 hours, by which time the acid had eaten right through the pewter (figure 108).

The mordant can be stored in a glass-stoppered bottle, marked POISON, and despite discolouration, can be used until it loses its strength.

Etching a Pendant

Materials and equipment

plain pewter pendant	a pan
candles	brush No 12
the traced design	etching tool
nitric acid	pyrex dish
cold water	tongs
hot water	feather
absorbent paper or rags	

This plain pendant was cast in cuttlefish bone. The reverse side and the edges were polished, but the front was left to show the texture of the cuttlebone.

Figure 109 : Equipment for etching

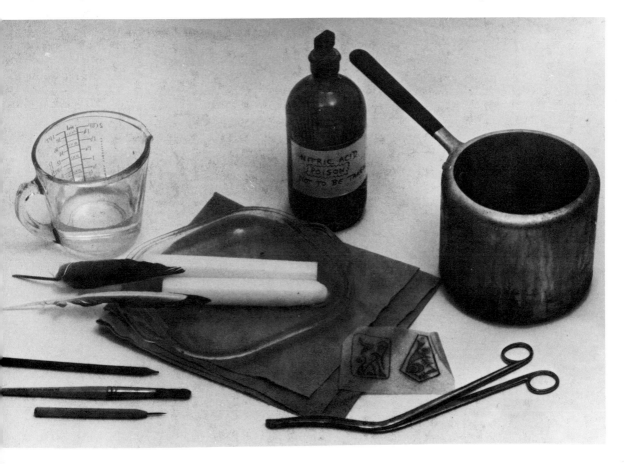

Method

(1) Melt the candle wax, and with a brush (size 12 holds plenty of wax) coat the pendant evenly on both sides and round the edges. Allow the wax to set, before painting on another coat. Four coats create a good etching ground and a favourable thickness upon which to work (figure 110).

(2) Place the traced design over the pendant and carefully draw the main lines to enable the rest to be completed freehand (figure 111).

(3) Using an etching tool, cut out the design and remove the wax from the areas which need to be exposed to the mordant. Care must be taken not to undercut or crack the wax. If it is possible to do this whilst the wax is still slightly warm it is less likely to crack (figure 112).

(4) Make sure that all loose particles of wax have been removed and that the wax is still intact around the vulnerable areas, such as the edges. If necessary, recoat any damaged places and then, with the help of a pair of tongs, immerse the pendant in the mordant (figure 113).

(5) Occasionally agitate the mordant to remove air bubbles which might form. Remove the pendant, rinse it in cold water and place it on an absorbent surface, in order to inspect it. If etching is slow, scratch the metal slightly to speed up the process before reimmersing. Repeat until the required result is achieved (figure 114).

Figure 110 : Painting on the fourth layer of candlewax

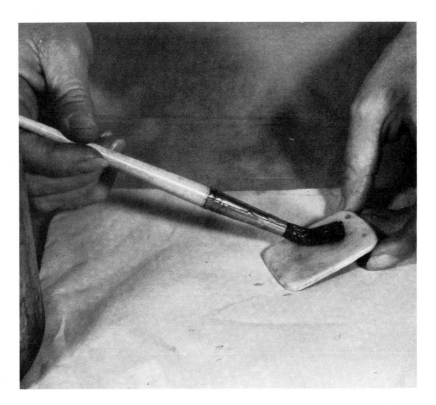

94

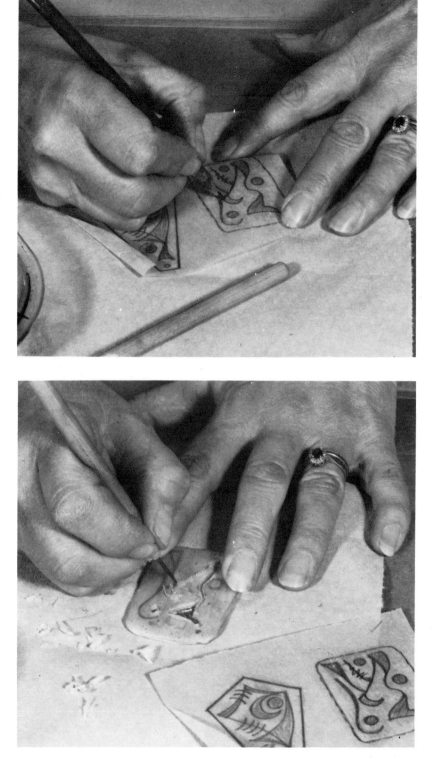

Figure 111 : Tracing the design onto the wax

Figure 112 : Using a sharp tool to cut out the design

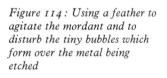

(6) Rinse with cold water after removing the pendant from the mordant and then melt the wax with hot water.

(7) Wash with hot soapy water and polish with grease remover until all the wax has been removed. Treat with patina if required (figure 115).

Figure 115 : The etched pendant

Correcting Faults

(1) If the wax cracks, it has probably been unevenly applied or carelessly handled.

(2) If an untidy, undefined edge occurs, it is because the etching tool undercut the wax and allowed the mordant to creep underneath it.

(3) Uneven etching is caused by air bubbles trapped in the acid, so ensure that the mordant is agitated. Loose particles of wax will also prevent the penetration of the acid.

(4) If the wax softens owing to heat caused by the acid, dilute the mordant by adding it to more water in another container.

*Figure 116 : Three etched
pendants : the natural cuttlefish
bone texture has been left on the
pendant in the centre, whilst the
two outer pendants were
polished to leave a smooth
finish*

Figure 117 : Designs for etched pendants

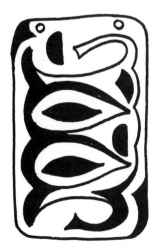

99

Soldering

Soldering Pewter

Soldering consists of joining pieces of metal together by flowing a molten alloy between them, and allowing it to solidify to form a whole.

Because of its low melting point, approximately 218.3°C to 226.6°C (425°F to 440°F), pewter is ideal for this type of work and can be soft soldered. Owing to the small content of oxide-producing metals (about 2% copper) in its composition, it requires no chemical cleaning after the soldering process. It also does not work harden, and therefore requires no annealing (that is, the process of heating and cooling the metal to make it less brittle).

The solder is an alloy of tin and lead, similar in colour to the pewter itself, with a melting point of approximately 170°C (370°F). The solder used must always have a lower melting point than the metal being soldered, otherwise the work would be damaged during heating. It is supplied in wire, strip, or sheet form, and can be easily cut with shears or snips into small pieces, known as paillons.

Just as every metal requires a special solder, it also needs a particular type of flux. In the case of pewter, proprietary brands can be used, although it is a simple matter to make one's own flux, by using 28 gm (1 oz) of glycerine to 7 drops of hydrochloric acid. Whilst mixing and for storage, it is advisable to keep the liquid in a glass-topped jar, the lid of which is invaluable for holding the paillons during working. Some authorities might suggest a greater amount of hydrochloric acid, but the higher the acid content, the greater the amount of residue left on the work. For applying the flux to the pewter, a sable brush No 5 is ideal. This must be perfectly dry because water and glycerine do not mix, and the flux would not flow evenly if water was present. The flux, when used correctly, produces a capillary attraction, and helps the molten solder to flow more easily.

Heat is applied by means of a flame or a soldering iron. There are numerous torches on the market, available through jeweller's suppliers, or from hardware and do-it-yourself shops, each with advantages and disadvantages. The choice is wide, so the factors to bear in mind are the available expenditure, and the various uses to which the torch or iron will be put. Very little heat is required to melt pewter, let alone the solder, so a fierce torch throwing out an excessively hot flame is not necessary.

The torch must be adjusted so that a steady, blue flame is produced. The tip of this is the hottest point, and it is this part of the flame which is directed onto the work.

When using an electric soldering iron, it is essential to use a small one, preferably one suitable for model making, otherwise the bit would be too clumsy to position accurately. The end of the iron, or bit, is made out of copper, which is set onto an iron rod or shank which connects with the handle. Only the tip of the copper comes into contact with the work.

Whilst soldering pewter, the amount of heat required is so small that the work can rest an asbestos mat. If, however, it is necessary to heat all round and underneath the work, then a soldering wig must be used. This is a circle of loosely compressed iron wire, attached to a handle which can be held by hand or balanced in a tripod for support.

A pair of tweezers is indispensable for arranging and adjusting the paillons and components. A cotton glove is quite thick enough for handling the work. Asbestos gloves tend to be far too clumsy for handling small work, although for larger articles, and for metals requiring greater heat, they are a worthwhile safety precaution.

Before starting to solder any article, it is essential to ensure that the hands, tools and the work space are clean and free from grease. If care is not taken to be scrupulously clean, the flux will probably not flow and the process will be disastrous. The parts to be soldered must be cleaned with either a degreasing agent, steel wool or soap and water and dried thoroughly. The bit of the soldering iron must be cleaned by filing away all traces of previous solder, which will remain as a thin coating on the end of the tool. It is important to switch off the electricity whilst doing this. Never allow the iron or hands to come into contact with water whilst the tool is 'live'.

Soldering a Pendant

Cast the shape for the pendant (figure 118) and the decorative components in pewter using the cuttlefish casting technique (figure 119).

Materials and equipment

solder	gloves
flux	shears or snips
gas torch	sharp knife
asbestos mat	file
no. 5 brush	hot soapy water
tweezers	
patina and cleaning materials (optional)	

Method

(1) To ensure that the solder is clean and free from impurities, strip it, that is scrape it with a sharp knife until it is bright and shiny (figure 121).
(2) Cut the solder into very small paillons of equal size with the shears, and allow them to fall into the lid of the glass jar. If desired, more than

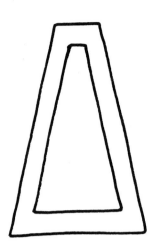  

Figure 118 : Designs for soldered pendants

Figure 119 : Components cast, ready for soldering

Figure 120 : Equipment for soldering

Figure 121 : Stripping the solder with a sharp knife

Figure 122 : Cutting the paillons

Figure 123: The paillons are filed to an even height after the first soldering, and the component is recoated with flux

one strip can be cut at the same time to obtain uniformity of size (figure 122).

(3) The process is more successful if paillons are soldered onto the components before placing them into their final positions. Coat the component with flux and heat the work until the flux begins to bubble. Remove the flame, otherwise it will dry before the paillons are placed into position. The boiling point of glycerine is 143.3°C (290°F), so the work will remain warm for a little while.

(4) Lift the flux-coated, cold, wet paillons with the brush and position them approximately 6 mm ($\frac{1}{4}$ in) apart on the warmed surface. If they do not adhere and partially melt, apply more heat, until the paillons form small mounds. Allow the work to cool, then file the top of the mounds flat and to an equal height, to allow the component to balance correctly before soldering it into its final position (figure 123).

(5) Continue the soldering process, that is coating with flux, heating the area, placing the paillons and allowing the solder to flow until each component is firmly in position (figure 124).

(6) Remove any residue from the flux by washing in warm, soapy water (figure 125).

(7) If an antique finish is required, immerse the pendant in patina and use the cleaning method described in the chapter on casting with cuttlefish.

Figure 125 : The completed pendant after washing away the residue in warm, soapy water

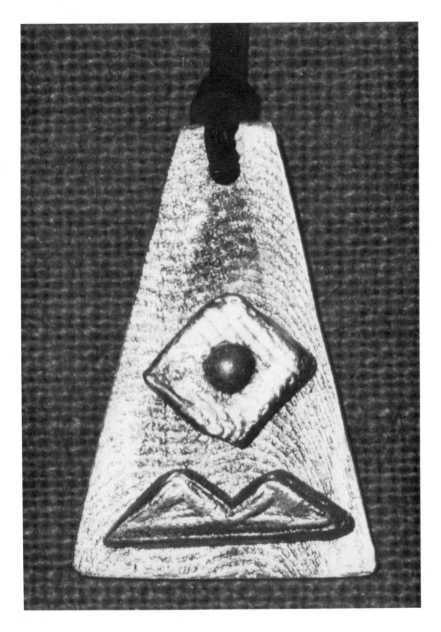

Figure 126 : A second pendant using the same idea

Soldering with an iron

When using an electric soldering iron, the order of the work is the same, but the heat is probably more difficult to control. The soldering bit, which is the tip of the iron, must be cleaned and tinned, that is covered with a layer of solder. Extreme caution must be taken to remove the bit as soon as the solder begins to flow, otherwise the pewter might be damaged.

Soldering is fun and providing the stages described are followed and the cleanliness rule adhered to, the results will be extremely rewarding.

Figure 127 : A pendant by Nigel Edmondson, cast in two pieces. The front section has been soldered onto the background, thereby giving greater depth to the design

Water-poured Pewter

Water-poured pewter is utterly unpredictable, and cannot be considered one hundred per cent durable, but it is fun to do.

As molten pewter is poured into a bucket of cold water, interesting shapes will form instantly. The pewter shown in figure 130 was poured from approximately 1 metre (3 feet) high. The longer the fall, the greater is the separation of the metal. Conversely, if the pouring takes place nearer to the water, the shapes produced are more solid.

Water-produced pewter can be soldered to form interesting pieces of jewellery, incorporating stones, or mounted onto other metals.

Figure 128 : Two soldered rings by Nigel Edmondson : (left) pewter and malachite ring and soldered sheet ; (right) a 'cylinder' ring using soldered pewter sheet

Figure 129: Water-poured pewter

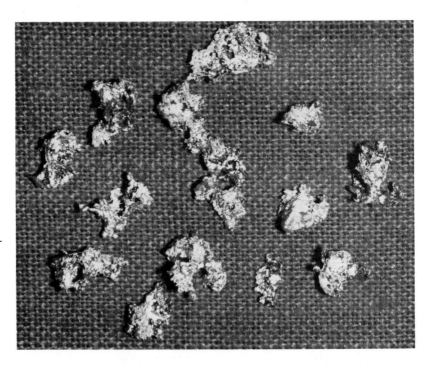

Figure 130: (Below left) Water-poured pewter soldered into position with an electric soldering iron, with two cabochons introduced to add colour. (Below right) The background and the scraps were flame heated and allowed to fuse together : both are experimental.

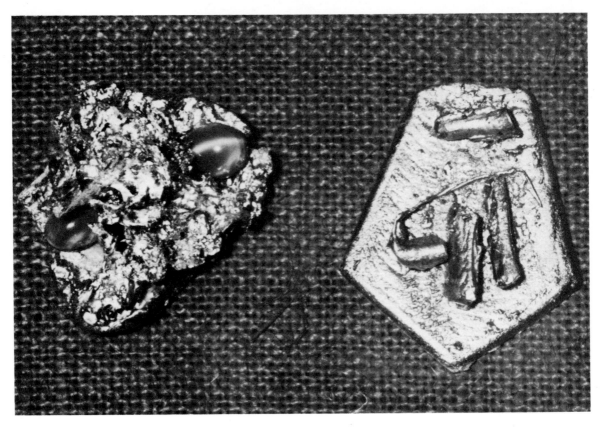

Appendices

Pewter Specifications

BSI BS 5140 1974 (British)

This alloy adheres strictly to the requirements laid down by the British Standards Institution.

Alloy	Sn	Sb	Cu	Pb	Cd
A	At least 91%	5–7	1–2.5	Max 0.5	Max 0.05
B	At least 93%	3–5	1–2.5	0.5	0.05

Other compositions are permitted provided Max Pb 0.5, Max Cd 0.05, and Sn not less than 91%. Elements other than Sn, Sb, Cu, Bi, Ni, Co, Ag shall not be more than 0.2%

DIN 17 810 1974 (German)

Alloy	Sn	Sb	Cu	Pb Max
2Sb 1½ Cu	Balance	1–3.0	1.0–2.0	0.5
5Sb 1½ Cu	Balance	3.1–7.0	1.0–2.0	0.5

Sn to specification DIN 1704 – 99.75% Sn
Sb 99.6% Sb
Cu to specification DIN 1708 – 99.90% Cu

ASTM B560 (American)

Type	Sn	Sb	Cu	Pb Max	As Max	Fe Max	Zn Max
1	90–91	6–8	0.25–2.0	0.05	0.05	0.015	0.005
2	90–93	5–7.5	1.5–3.0	0.05	0.05	0.015	0.005
3	95–98	1.0–3.0	1.0–2.0	0.05	0.05	0.015	0.005

Density 7.3   Liq 295°C   Sol 244°C

Table of Melting Points

	Symbol	Degrees Centigrade	Degrees Fahrenheit
Aluminium	Al	659.7	1219.6
Antimony	Sb	630.5	1166.9
Arsenic	As	814*	1497*
Bismuth	Bi	271.3	520.3
Cadmium	Cd	320.9	609.62
Cobalt	Co	1480	2696
Copper	Cu	1083	1981.4
Gold	Au	1063	1945.4
Iron	Fe	1535	2795
Lead	Pb	327.4	621.32
Nickel	Ni	1455	2650.8
Silver	Ag	960.5	1760.9
Tin	Sn	231.89	449.42
Zinc	Zn	419.47	787.04

*At 36 atmospheres ie 36 times atmospheric pressure.

Conversion of Measurements

Fahrenheit to Centigrade

From the number of degrees Fahrenheit, subtract 32. Multiply the result by 5 and divide by 9.

Centigrade to Fahrenheit

Multiply the number of degrees Centigrade by 9. Divide by 5 and add 32.

Capacity

1 fluid ounce = 1 ounce avoirdupois = 28.417 cu cm = 0.0284123 litre.

Cabochon Sizes

Dimensions vary slightly with each supplier but this list is a rough guide to the sizes of cabochons available.

Round	Oval
5 mm ($\frac{3}{16}$ in)	7 by 5 mm ($\frac{1}{4} \times \frac{3}{16}$ in)
7 mm ($\frac{1}{4}$ in)	10 by 8 mm ($\frac{1}{8} \times \frac{5}{16}$ in)
8 mm ($\frac{5}{16}$ in)	14 by 10 mm ($\frac{5}{8} \times \frac{3}{8}$ in)
10 mm ($\frac{3}{8}$ in)	16 by 12 mm ($\frac{5}{8} \times \frac{1}{2}$ in)
12 mm ($\frac{1}{2}$ in)	18 by 13 mm ($\frac{3}{4} \times \frac{1}{2}$ in)
15 mm ($\frac{5}{8}$ in)	22 by 12 mm ($\frac{7}{8} \times \frac{1}{2}$ in)
18 mm ($\frac{3}{4}$ in)	25 by 18 mm ($1 \times \frac{3}{4}$ in)
	40 by 30 mm ($1\frac{1}{2} \times 1\frac{1}{8}$ in)

Birthday Stones

January	*garnet*
February	*amethyst*
March	*aquamarine or heliotrope (bloodstone)*
April	*diamond, zircon or rock crystal*
May	*emerald, chrysoprase or green-dyed chalcedony*
June	*pearl or moonstone*
July	*ruby or carnelian*
August	*peridot or sardonyx*
September	*sapphire or lapis lazuli*
October	*opal or tourmaline*
November	*topaz or citrine*
December	*turquoise*

Tenth wedding anniversary

The traditional gift for the tenth wedding anniversary is an item made from tin. There is a growing tendency to give pewter for this celebration.

Acids

They are most easily obtained through laboratory reagent suppliers (especially those catering for schools). The analytical quality has no advantage over the commercial variety which of course is much cheaper.

The acids are usually supplied in a concentrated form, unless special instructions are given for them to be supplied diluted. This latter procedure is naturally more expensive, and providing care is taken, there is no reason why the concentrated acids should not be diluted with safety.

It is important to remember that nitric acid is very corrosive and will quickly damage skin, and therefore all utensils and the bottle itself should be carefully wiped over to remove traces after use. Additionally, nitric acid produces a brown gas, nitrogen peroxide, especially when in contact with certain metals such as tin and copper. This gas is intensely irritating to the tissues of the eyes and lungs.

Hydrochloric acid, or Spirits of Salts as it is known commercially, is also corrosive and gives off chlorine gas, which again is irritating and harmful to lung tissues. Always handle with care and use in a well ventilated area.

Wax

There are three main types of wax which may be categorized into the following groups:

(1)   Hydrocarbon group
(2)   Natural ester group
(3)   Synthetic group.

The properties of beeswax, which belongs to the natural ester group, vary widely owing to the fact that it is a natural animal excretion and its source of origin can vary its composition considerably. Synthetic waxes are sometimes mixed with beeswax to produce less variable properties.

Synthetic wax, now widely used in casting, is more predictable and constant. One should be able to carve it, using various craft knives and sharp tools, without the wax flaking or cracking. A smooth surface can be obtained by either heating a knife over a spirit lamp, or by using an electrically heated knife and smoothing it over the model. The more accurate the wax carving is, the fewer are the finishing processes required to perfect the end product.

Investment materials

It is essential to follow the instructions carefully. When mixing, the material should form a smooth consistency, the particle size being small enough to give a surface smoothness to the mould when the wax has been removed.

It should have a predictable setting time and it should not crack or decompose when in contact with the molten metal.

On no account should one be tempted to use a cheap substitute such as plaster of Paris, because this will not stand the heat of molten metal.

First Aid

Acids

It is mandatory for acids to be supplied in dark, fluted, glass-stoppered bottles, clearly marked POISON, NOT TO BE TAKEN, CORROS-IVE. Always add ACID TO WATER, not the other way round. Use in a well ventilated area and take precautions against splashes. In the event of splashing the eyes and face, the quickest first aid measure is to immerse the head in a plastic bucket of bicarbonate solution. Usually no permanent harm results from diluted acids, but in the case of a severe burn to the eye, medical attention should be sought immediately.

Burns

Slight burns should be coated with a proprietary cream or spray (such as Acriflavin) and covered with a dry, sterile dressing. Burns caused by molten metal can be serious and medical attention should be sought immediately. In the meantime cover with a dry, sterile dressing.

Cuts and bleeding

People using tools should have tetanus injections every five years. Minor cuts and abrasions can be cleaned with an antiseptic solution (such as TCP or liquid Savlon) before applying a bandage. Severe cuts should receive medical attention. If ever in doubt get in touch with a doctor as soon as possible.

Bibliography

Books

Anglo Saxon Jewellery, Ronald Jessup (Faber)
Cast Pewter Jewelry, Joy D Kain (Davis Publications Inc, New York; Ward Lock Ltd, London)
Catalogue of Medieval Antiquities 1977, Library of The Museum of London
Cutting and Setting Stones, Herbert Scarfe (Batsford)
Design and Form, Johannes Itten (Thames & Hudson)
Design by Accident, James F O'Brien (Dover Publications Inc, New York)
Design Lessons from Nature, Benjamin and Debbie Taylor (Pitman)
Engraving on Precious Metals, A Brittain (NAG Press 1953)
Ideas for Jewelry, Ian Davidson (Batsford)
Illustrated Dictionary of Jewellery, Mason and Packer (Osprey Publications)
Introducing Jewelry Making, John Crawford (Batsford)
Jewels of the Pharaohs, Cyril Aldred (Thames & Hudson)
Metalwork, Hans Ulrich Haedeke (Weidenfeld and Nicolson)
Metalwork and Enamelling, Herbert Maryon (Dover Publications, New York)
Modern Pewter Designs and Technique, Shirley Charron (David & Charles)
New Designs in Jewelry, Donald Willcox (Van Nostrand Reinhold)
Samenas Konstskatter, Istvan Racz (Sweden)
Technique of Jewellery, Rod Edwards (Batsford)
The Folk Arts of Norway, Janice S Steward (Dover Publications Inc, New York)

Leaflets

Pewter published by the International Tin Research Institute, Publication No 494
Tin and its Uses published by the International Tin Research Institute, publication No 106, 1975
Craft Education No 38, Autumn Term 1975
Investment Lost Wax Casting by J P P Jones and D E Harper (Heinemann Educational Books Ltd, available from W J Hooker Ltd)
Tandem Casting Alloys for Jewellery and Model Making No J1 and *Solder and Fluxes* No 1, Technical Publications from Fry's Metals Ltd
Notes on the History of The Pewterers' Company obtainable from the Worshipful Company of Pewterers

List of Suppliers

UK

Thin Pewter Sheet

Fred Aldous
37 Lever Street
Manchester M60 1UX

Kernocraft
21 Pydar Street
Truro
Cornwall TR1 2AY

Southern Handicrafts Ltd
25 Kensington Gardens
Brighton BN1 4AL

Pewter and Solder

George Johnson & Co
Birmingham Ltd
Highlands Road
Shirley
Solihull
West Midlands

The Old Park Silver Mills Co Ltd
Club Mill Road
Sheffield S6 2FF

Fry's Metals Ltd
Tandem Works
Merton Abbey
London SW19 2PD

Tools

Charles Cooper (Hatton Garden) Ltd
Knights House
23–27 Hatton Wall
Hatton Garden
London EC1N 8JJ

E Gray & Son Ltd
12–16 Clerkenwell Road
London EC1

A G Thomas (Bradford) Ltd
Dept J M Tompion House
Heaton Road
Bradford BD8 8RB

Stones

Pebblegems
71 St Marks Road
Bush Hill Park
Enfield
Middlesex EN1 1BH

Abbeygems Products
PO Box 35
Waltham Cross
Herts EN8 7JZ

Casting Materials

W J Hooker Ltd
Waterside
Brightlingsea
Essex

Cuttlefish bone

Charles Cooper (Hatton Gdn) Ltd
Knights House
23–27 Hatton Wall
Hatton Garden
London EC1N 8JJ

Acids

Hopkin & Williams
Chemicals & Reagents
PO Box 1
Romford RM1 1HA

Information

International Tin Research Institute
Fraser Road
Greenford
Middlesex UB6 7AQ

The Worshipful Company of Pewterers
Pewterers Hall
Oat Lane
London EC2V 7DE

USA

Metals, tools

Allcraft
22 West 48th Street
New York, NY 10036

American Handicraft Co Inc
20 West 14th Street
New York, NY 10011

Anchor Tool & Supply Co Inc
12 John Street
New York, NY 10038

DRS
110 West 47th Street
New York, NY 10036

C R Hill Co
2734 West 11 Mile Road
Berkley
Michigan 48072

Marshall-Swartchild Co
2040 Milwaukee Avenue
Chicago
Illinois 60657

C W Somers & Co
387 Washington Street
Boston
Massachusetts 02108

Francis Hoover
12445 Chandler Blvd
North Hollywood
California 91607

International Gem Co
15 Maiden Lane
New York, NY 10038

Nathan Gem and Pearl Co Inc
18 East 48th Street
New York, NY 10017

Findings

Hagstoz and Son
709 Sansom Street
Philadelphia
Pennsylvania 19106

Krieger and Dranoff
44 West 47th Street
New York, NY 10036

Stones

John Barry Co
Department C
PO Box 15
Detroit
Michigan 48231

AUSTRALIA

Australian Silvercraft Centre
104 Bathurst Street
Sydney, NSW 2000

Campbell's Gemstones
324 South Road
Moorabbin, Victoria 3189

Contemporary Crafts and Supplies
Cnr Gladstone Road & Dorchester Street
Highgate Hill, Queensland 4101

Fordell Supplies
83 York Street
Sydney, NSW 2000

Handcraft Metals
40 Atchinson Street
St Leonards, NSW 2065

Pat Brown-Eklund
PO Box 34
French's Forest, NSW 2086

Index